For Fern,
    With love and
Thanksgiving in
the Lord.
        Donna

PS
Some of this is
pretty tough but I
know you'll still love me!

Life
Along
the Way

DONNA LEWIS ABRAMS

WESTBOW
PRESS®
A DIVISION OF THOMAS NELSON
& ZONDERVAN

All scripture quotes are from the King James version of the Bible.

WestBow Press books may be ordered through booksellers or by contacting:

WestBow Press
A Division of Thomas Nelson & Zondervan
1663 Liberty Drive
Bloomington, IN 47403
www.westbowpress.com
1 (866) 928-1240

ISBN: 978-1-5127-8139-7 (sc)
ISBN: 978-1-5127-8138-0 (hc)
ISBN: 978-1-5127-8137-3 (e)

Library of Congress Control Number: 2017904554

Print information available on the last page.

WestBow Press rev. date: 05/03/2017

Thank you, Lord, for your Life. Thank you, Linda, my sister twice, for your love and encouragement. Thank you, precious brothers and sisters in Christ, for putting up with me all these years, for instructing me in the gospel, and growing me in Jesus by your love and example.

Contents

1

A Sent Word

Second Timothy 3:16 says that all scripture is given by inspiration of God, and is profitable for doctrine, for reproof, for correction, for instruction in righteousness.

Jesus says in John 14:26, "But the Comforter, which is the Holy Ghost, whom the Father will send in My name, He shall teach you all things, and *bring all things to your remembrance,* whatsoever I have said unto you."

How wonderful it is when the Holy Spirit brings a scripture to you that just fits the situation in which you find yourself. This is the reason we need to read the scriptures consistently on a daily basis. Will He bring to your remembrance what you have never read? Possibly, but it is more likely to happen if you have read it.

There have been many times when the Lord sent a scripture to help me when I was in a rough spot. One I remember well happened during the years I was taking care of both my parents. It was near Christmas. My mother wanted to go to Macy's. She was not in the wheelchair yet, but close to needing one, as her knees were caving in with arthritis. Walking was a slow and painful process.

The parking lot was crowded, but I saw a man in a handicap spot putting a wheelchair in a van. We had a handicap sticker, so I pulled up near him, turned on my blinker indicating I wanted his parking spot, and waited.

There was a car parked in front of Macy's at the entrance. The car had no blinker on, so I supposed the two young men and child in it were waiting to pick up someone coming out of the store.

When the van left, I pulled into the handicap space. I got out just as the car parked in front of Macy's sped by with the driver shouting. I couldn't hear what he was saying, but a lady walking by said to me, "Did you hear what he was saying to you? He was threatening you." I had not heard specifics due to the sound of the car motor. I thought that was the end of it, but not so.

I helped Mother out of the car and into the store. No sooner were we inside when I was confronted by a raging man six inches from my face. He was livid, screaming that I had taken his parking place. I told him I was sorry that I had not realized he wanted it, as I saw no blinker flashing and thought he was parked at the entrance to pick someone up. I pointed to my mother, who was standing there frightened and wide-eyed.

The man continued swearing and yelling; then a scripture leaped into my mind, "A soft answer turneth away wrath" (Proverbs 15:1). Boy, this was surely the right time to try that!

Looking into his angry face, I said, "I will pray for you and ask God to forgive you for the way you are speaking to one of His children." His shoulders slumped. His demeanor changed, and he told me to forget it, as he walked away to join his very embarrassed friend and child.

What a wonderful thing when the Lord sends His word into a situation! There are no formulas when walking with the Lord. If we abide in the vine, read the scriptures, and yield our lives to Him, then we can know more and more what it is like to "live and move and have our being in Him" (Acts 17:28). He will "send" His word, just the one we need, and at just the right time.

2

Afterward

In John 13:33-38, Jesus was preparing His disciples for His soon-coming departure. He told them He was going away. They would seek Him, but would not be able to find Him, that is, not until afterward. Of course, we know Peter vowed he would follow and even lay down his life for the Lord. His intentions were noteworthy, but Peter needed an "afterward" in his life. We all do.

The events would fall into place with the precision of eternal design: the garden, the betrayal, the arrest, the mocking, the torture, the denials, the crucifixion, death, and burial. Then, oh yes, then the afterward: resurrection, ascension, coming of the Holy Spirit, and finally, His return as King of Kings and Lord of Lords. Oh, the blessedness of the "afterward"!

Our lives are made up of seasons spent waiting for the "afterward" of events in which we find ourselves. We experience this and wonder about that. Sometimes we discover the "afterward" in this life. Sometimes we will not, until eternity removes the darkened glass completely, and we see face to face. However, and whenever, the Lord *will* give us understanding in all things.

In Hebrews 12:11 scripture tells us, "Now ... no chastening for the present seemeth to be joyous, but grievous, nevertheless *afterward,* it yieldeth the peaceable fruit of righteousness unto them which are exercised thereby." Afterward comes the fruit. God is more concerned with our fruit than with our comfort. His eye is set on His purpose in the "afterward".

Jesus certainly had His determination grounded in the "afterward". Scripture tells us in Hebrews 12:2 that "for the joy that was set before Him, He endured the cross." He saw the afterward that was coming! He was able to endure the horror of it all because He knew what was coming afterward ... He would bring many sons and daughters to glory! Redemption would be completed for humankind!

However much we scream, complain, resist, weep, and demand, God is still bent on "afterward". He knows how to make His servants stand and is relentless in doing so. For us to be in the great company of overcomers, there must be something in life to overcome.

When we do not understand the circumstances in which we find ourselves, or those we love, when we are swimming in deep waters, gasping and hardly staying afloat, we do well to remember Proverbs 29:11, which reads... "A fool uttereth all his mind, but a wise man keepeth it till *afterwards."* Be still and know that He is God. There will be an *afterward*!

3

As They Went

In Luke 17:11-19, Jesus was journeying to Jerusalem when He met ten men who were lepers. They were standing afar off, as required by law. When they knew it was Jesus passing by, they cried out to Him for mercy. When Jesus saw them, He did not speak healing to them, or forgive their sins. In verse 14, scripture says, "And when He saw them, He said unto them, 'Go show yourselves unto the priests.' And it came to pass, that, *as they went they were cleansed.*"

These lepers went on a word from Jesus, and they were healed as they went. He *sent* His word and healed them. There has to be a sending of the word. We can never rule out the Living Word sending the written word. When the Living Word sends the written word, there is always creation.

Where we often bring confusion is when we try to implement the written word apart from the Living Word. It's like holding a plug in our hand near the wall socket without inserting it into the wall; no connection, no power. We need both, for the Living Word, Jesus, has fulfilled the written word and has been exalted above all. He is the Word of God!

In Mark 12:1-11, Jesus gives the parable of the husbandmen. A man planted a vineyard, left it in charge of husbandmen, and went into a far country. He sent a series of servants to check on the fruit. These servants were beaten and mistreated. At last he sent his son, expecting the husbandmen to respect him. However, they killed the son and seized his inheritance for themselves. Jesus said the owner of the vineyard would come, destroy the husbandmen, and give the vineyard to others.

Of course, we know Jesus spoke this parable concerning the Jews and Himself. They would reject prophets and Him, thus opening the door of salvation for the Gentiles. There is a powerful word, however, spoken to us all in verse 7. Jesus said of them, "This is the heir, come let us kill him and the inheritance shall be ours." Disregard Jesus and try to seize the inheritance. Attempts to live in the inheritance without the Life of the Living Word can be disastrous.

Jesus speaks more about this in Matthew 7:21-23, where He said, "Not every one that saith unto Me, 'Lord, Lord,' shall enter into the kingdom of heaven, but he that doeth the will of My Father which is in heaven. Many will say to Me in that day, Lord, Lord, have we not prophesied in Thy name and in Thy name cast out devils and in Thy name done many wonderful works?' And then will I profess unto them, *I never knew you*. Depart from Me, ye that work iniquity.'"

What a serious word from the Lord is that! Power demonstrated to heal and deliver apart from the Living Word will end in disaster. Not only will seizing the inheritance apart from Christ end in disaster, but it will also be placed in the column with iniquity. You cannot separate the Living Word from the written word.

One leper, only one, knew this. He was the only one who returned to the Source of his healing, falling down on his face before Jesus, giving Him praise and thanks. And this one was a Samaritan.

There are several statements in scripture that are very sad to me, and the response of Jesus here in verse 17 is one of them. He said simply, "Were there not ten cleansed? Where are the other nine?" One in ten gave God the glory; one in ten. One in ten did not take the Son's inheritance without forgetting Him; one in ten.

4

Baptized with Fire

In Luke 3:15-17, scripture tells us that people were in expectation and mused in their heads if John were the Christ, or not. They were expecting the Messiah. They were looking with anticipation for Him, even if their expectations were more in the line of a natural king. John set the record straight in verses 16 and 17 when he answered by saying, "I indeed baptize you with water; but one mightier than I cometh, the latchet of whose shoes I am not worthy to unloose; He shall baptize you with the Holy Ghost and with *fire*, whose fan is in His hand, and He will thoroughly purge His floor, and will gather the wheat into His garner; but the chaff He will burn with fire unquenchable."

Most Christians accept the baptism with the Holy Ghost, but they don't like the sound of the *fire*. Everyone knows the awful pain of being burned. Fire destroys. It defaces. It darkens the scene. We prefer the coolness of water, the lovely, beautiful symbolism of being buried with Jesus in death and raised into His life.

Jesus spoke about this subject in Matthew 20:18-28. He had just talked to the disciples again about what was going to happen to Him in Jerusalem. One would think after such a serious discussion, the topic of conversation would not be about their personal greatness. However, it was. Verse 20 and forward reads:

> "Then came to Him the mother of Zebedee's children with her sons, worshipping Him, and desiring a certain thing of Him. And He said unto her, 'What will thou?' She saith unto Him, 'Grant that these my two sons, may sit, the one on Thy right hand, and the other on Thy left, in Thy kingdom.' But Jesus answered and said, 'Ye know not what ye ask. Are ye able to drink of the cup that I shall drink of and to be baptized with the baptism that I am baptized with?'"

He certainly wasn't talking about plain water here, but something far more difficult than immersion. Jesus had already been baptized in water by John the Baptist. The baptism He spoke of here was not of water, but of fire.

The fire that Jesus was about to experience was submission to God's will carried out through the hands of men influenced and energized by the Prince of Darkness. He would endure the fire of the cross for the joy that was set before Him. We can endure our own fire by experiencing that same joy in seeing Him who is invisible, living and moving and having our being in Him (Acts 17:28).

The fire is not predictable. We cannot ignite it ourselves. We can only acknowledge that we have wood, hay, and stubble, and trust our Lord to send the forces to destroy them (1 Corinthians 3:12-15). If we belong to Jesus, He will burn the wood, hay, and stubble, either in this life with the promise of reward, or in the next with the suffering of loss. Either way, the fire will do its work.

5

Bearing with Jesus

The loss of my husband was a shock…two weeks of illness, then he was gone. Living on a farm in the dead of winter meant contending with hay, feed, and frozen water. Then there was the selling of livestock, tractors, equipment, machinery, tools, and all items farm-related. All the while, I was sole caregiver to my live-in father, who was in his nineties.

To my surprise, the farm did not sell quickly. In fact, almost three years passed, and there we sat. I was still caring for Dad and fretting over pastures that had to be mowed and fence lines that needed spraying. I was stressed and weary of dealing with a full plate day after day. I was tired of preparing the farm and house for viewing, only to be disappointed again with a " no sale".

Fatigue set in, coupled with frustration and tears. Health issues arose that had no definitive conclusions. The heart checked out fine, waning kidney function improved, and lumps turned out to be only lipomas. The problem seemed to lie elsewhere.

One morning, July 8, 2015, precious Jesus spoke to me, and that changed everything. I had my usual morning time of reading the

Bible and some devotional books, then went out on my front porch to pray. After some tears and mostly murmuring, the Lord spoke to my heart. It wasn't profound or other worldly. He simply said, "Bear with Me a little longer." That was it. Yet, the speaking of it enlarged in my heart and mind. As always, when the Lord speaks, there is creation. Within His speaking, and my receiving, lay the strengthening I needed to carry on.

Immediately, I thought of His words to the disciples in the upper room as they prepared for Passover and His crucifixion. He told them in John 16:12, "I have yet many things to say unto you, but ye cannot bear them now." I thought of the garden in Gethsemane when He asked them the question, "Could ye not watch *with Me* one hour?" (Matthew 26:40).

At the Passover supper, He stated a fact: they could not bear, and He knew it. In Gethsemane, however, He asked a question, "*Will you* watch with Me?" There is a difference.

His word to me, "Bear with me a little longer," was an imploration to continue in earnest, knowing there would come an end to the present trial. How great is that! How great is that to have a personal relationship with the Saviour ... to hear His voice, whether in instruction, comfort, rebuke, exhortation, or, imploration. How great is that!

Jesus understands weary. Remember, He napped in the boat, His head resting on a pillow. He sat by the well weary, waiting while His disciples went to town for provisions.

Jesus knows when we need those "times of refreshing from the presence of the Lord" (Acts 3:19). He knows just when to "confirm His inheritance when it is weary" (Psalm 68:9).

As I type this, six months have passed since that morning. There have been more prospective buyers who did not buy, more work on the farm, and a worsening of Dad's health issues. However, I am continuing to bear with Jesus and resting in James 5:11, which says, "Behold, we count them happy which endure."

As a postscript, my dear Dad did not want to die and leave me alone on the farm. On April 13, 2016, my farm sold. Two days later, my father passed into glory. God is faithful. He waited in order to be gracious unto me, as a house just suited for my needs was put on the market a few days before I went house hunting.

6

Behold a Mystery

On the cross in excruciating pain and suffering, Jesus forgave those who were crucifying Him, asking the Father to forgive them, for they didn't know what they were doing.

It is a different Jesus in the temple, however. He went so far in His zeal that He made a whip, drove out the sacrificial animals, poured out the money changers' coins, and overthrew their tables. He declared His Father's house was a house of prayer, not one of merchandizing (Mark 11:15-17). He did this with energy, great passion, and heart intent.

Lest we think this demonstration was without restraint and done on impulse, we need to remember that Jesus had visited this same temple the day before, certainly saw all that was going on there, yet did nothing. It was the following day that He returned and moved with passion to cleanse His Father's house (Mark 11:11, 15). Jesus never acted on impulse, but was always in the Spirit and following the Father's directive.

The disciples remembered that it was written of Him that the zeal of thine house hath eaten Me up. (John 2: 17). Jesus had tremendous respect, deep honor, and a holy regard for His Father's house, which at that time was represented by the temple in Jerusalem. The temple stood as the place of contact between God and His people. It was to be treated with reverence and awe.

In Ephesians 5:22-33 Paul goes into great detail about the marriage relationship between a man and a woman. After doing so, he makes one of the greatest proclamations in scripture in verse 32. Paul says, "This is a great mystery but I (in speaking about marriage between a man and a woman) speak concerning Christ and the Church."

In that one sentence, Paul, under divine inspiration of the Holy Spirit, gathered all that Jesus came to do, was, and is to come, and cemented it into one holy comparison: it is like the marriage between a man and his wife. Therein lies the great mystery.... a mystery of comparison that is to be respected, honored, celebrated, and feared.

No wonder Satan hurls such an attack at marriage. It is not just God-ordained marriage between man and woman that he is after. He is after the mystery... the great mystery that Paul spoke of when he compared marriage between a man and a woman to that of Christ and His church. Satan knows what that represents, and He hates it. He reaches out to influence man to defile the holiest, most sacred union that the Lord gave Himself to establish: His union with His bride, the church.

Oh, we need to be careful with this great mystery. We need to hold it in highest regard. Jesus demonstrated His passion in temple cleansing. How do you think He feels about this?

7

Big Experience

In John 3:34, scripture speaks of Jesus saying, "For He whom God hath sent speaketh the words of God for God giveth not the Spirit by measure unto Him." Jesus, of course, had not the Spirit in part but the whole. He was the embodiment of God Himself, the fullness of God, the express image of His person. He told His disciples, "If you have seen Me, you have seen the Father" (John 14:9).

Christians, however, are told in 2 Corinthians 1:22 and 5:5 that we have been given the "earnest" of the Spirit. The earnest is the assurance, the pledge, the promise, the indication of what is to follow. The earnest has been paid by the buyer to the seller to bind the transaction. We are bought with a price. We are not our own anymore.

By position we have all in Christ. By experience, however, we are working out our salvation with fear and trembling (Philippians 2:12). When we no longer age or die, and when we can walk through a door without opening it like Jesus did, then we will know that our experience has caught up with our position!

Ephesians 1:13-14 reads:

"In whom ye also trusted, after that ye heard the word of truth, the gospel of your salvation: in whom also after that ye believed, ye were sealed with that holy Spirit of promise, which is the earnest of our inheritance until the redemption of the purchased possession, unto the praise of His glory."

We wait for that big experience... the redemption of the purchased possession.

As we follow on to know the Lord, not just His power, as we grow in grace and in the *knowledge of Him*, we should be leaving milk and eating meat (Hebrews 5:13-14, 6:1-3). We should be entering more into the realm of His life in which we find ourselves "living, and moving and having our being" in Him (Acts 17:28).

In His *life* we taste the good word of God and the power of the world to come (Hebrews 6:5). However, we must realize that we "have this treasure in earthen vessels that the excellency of the power may be of God and not of us" (2 Corinthians 4:7). The danger comes in thinking the power is ours to wield at our own discretion and not by the initiation of God. If we knew such kingdom power at this present time in earthly vessels, there would be only wreck and ruin. We don't have to look far in the past to see examples of this in the lives of those who claimed to have such power.

Remember that Jesus had trouble with some of His own disciples who wanted to exercise power. They rejoiced over the power to cast out demons. Jesus responded by telling them to rejoice that their names were written in heaven, not in power over demons. Some wanted to send fire down to consume those who refused Him lodging. He told them they did not know what spirit they were of. Some wanted to be esteemed the "greatest" and sit on His right and left in His kingdom. He told them the greatest among them would be those that serve.

Power minus the "yoke" equals disaster. The yoke, of course, being one with Christ. He says in Matthew 11:28-29 that taking His yoke upon you will result in learning that He is meek and lowly in heart, and subsequently, you will find rest in your soul. Attempting to use the power and authority of God without being yoked with Christ results in the way of truth being evil spoken of (2 Peter 2:1-2). In fact, the whole of chapter two in 2 Peter is full of such warning. Too often the power of God is equated with the power of men being expressed with force or loud demanding authority. Where is the meekness and lowliness in heart in that? Demons know the difference between God's authority and man's imitation of such, even if accompanied by the quoting of scripture.

God certainly knew what He was doing when He gave us the "earnest" of the spirit until these bodies are changed like unto His glorious body and He subdues all things unto Himself (Philippians 3:21). Hebrews 2:8-9 explains clearly that all things have been put under His feet, but *we see not yet* all things put under Him; but we see Jesus crowned with glory and honor. When we, or our loved one, is seriously ill, we pray, we believe; if there is healing, we rejoice; if there is no healing, we *still see Jesus crowned with glory and honor!*

Obviously, there remains something more to happen, or the aging process would not exist, nor would sickness or death. We who have the earnest of the spirit are waiting, watching, and listening for the sound of the trumpet … "for this corruptible *must put on incorruption, and this mortal must put on immortality.* So when this corruptible shall have put on incorruption, and this mortal shall have put on immortality, *then shall be brought to pass* the saying that is written, 'Death is swallowed up in victory!'" (I Corinthians 15:53-54).

Until that glorious day when we see all things put under His feet and are changed into His likeness, having a body like His; until then we "taste" of the powers of the world to come. We have glimpses, wonderful glimpses, seeing through a glass darkly, but then, when we are changed and that which is perfect is come, we shall see face to face, not in part. We shall know even as we are known (1 Corinthians 13:12).

His grace is sufficient to carry us through until, indeed, mortality is swallowed up of life (2 Corinthians 5:4). Then and only then, will our experience be completely united with our position. Then and only then, will the kingdom of God not just be within but also without. Christ will be all in all! What a day that will be!

8

Brought Nigh by the Blood, not Doctrine

D octrine: (1) something taught; teachings (2) something taught as the principles or creed of a religion, political party, tenet or tenets; belief; dogma

In 2 Timothy 3:16-17, the Bible says, *"All scripture* is given by inspiration of God and is *profitable for doctrine,* for reproof, for correction, for instruction in righteousness that the man of God may be perfect, thoroughly furnished unto all good works."

All scripture is profitable for doctrine, for teaching as principles, or creeds of Christian faith. Therefore, you may select any number of scriptures to practice in your assembly, or exclude from your assembly. The field is wide open: immersion in water, sprinkling, spiritual gifts, foot washing, head covering, pastors, elders, deacons, women speaking or remaining silent, tithing or cheerful giving, apostles and prophets or no apostles and prophets, communion every Sunday or as oft as you will, musical instruments or acapella. The list could go on and on.

However, the scripture is emphatic on *one overriding principle*: we are brought nigh unto God by the *blood of Jesus Christ* and nothing else. *This is the gospel of God.* This is *the doctrine* that supersedes all others.

In Ephesians 2:13-19, we read:

> "But now in Christ Jesus ye who sometimes were far off are made nigh by the blood of Christ. For He is our peace, who hath broken down the middle wall of partition between us; having abolished in His flesh the enmity, even the law of commandments contained in ordinances; for to make in Himself of twain one new man, so making peace; And that He might reconcile both unto God in one body by the cross, having slain the enmity thereby: And came and preached peace to you which were afar off, and to them that were nigh. For *through Him we both have access by one Spirit unto the* Father."

Acceptance before God, and fellowship with one another, centers around this bedrock belief and nothing else. If you believe that Jesus Christ is the Son of God, conceived by the Holy Spirit, born of a virgin, lived a sinless life, was crucified, died, rose again on the third day, ascended back to heaven where He sits exalted on the right hand of God, ever living to make intercession for the saints, waiting to come to earth a second time to establish His kingdom and fill all in all, then, you are a Christian. You have been brought nigh to God by His Son's precious blood and not the keeping of a particular doctrine, however scriptural that doctrine may be.

Paul discussed spiritual gifts (not talents) and ministries within the body of Christ in 1 Corinthians 12. He summed up the differences people were having concerning these things by stressing in verses 13 and 14, "For by one Spirit are we all baptized into one body, whether we be Jews or Gentiles, whether we be bond or free; and have been all made to drink into one Spirit. For the body is not one member, but many."

Again, Paul says in verses 25 through 27:

> "That there should be no schism in the body; but that the members should have the same care one for another. And whether one member suffer, all the members suffer with it; or one member be honored, all the members rejoice with it. Now ye are the body of Christ, and members in particular."

The body of Christ needs all its members. The arm can't tell the foot, "I don't need you." The ear can't tell the eye, "I don't need you." Those who practice the gifts of the Spirit need those who do not. The head covering wearers need the once-a-week communion takers. Those who immerse need those who sprinkle. Those who raise hands and shout need those who quietly sit and pray silently. Those who wash feet at communion need those who do not.

Paul so beautifully expressed in Ephesians 4:3 that we should endeavor to keep the unity of the Spirit in the bond of peace. He stressed that there is one body, one Spirit, one Lord, one faith, one baptism, one God and Father of all.

Paul spoke of the purpose of the fivefold ministries of apostles, prophets, evangelists, pastors, and teachers being the instruments through which the Lord would bring us into the unity of the faith and of the knowledge of the Son of God, to a perfect man, to the measure of the stature of the fullness of Christ.

Paul warned in verse 14 about being "tossed to and fro and carried about with every wind of doctrine, by the sleight of men and cunning craftiness whereby they lie in wait to deceive."

Finally, in verses 15 and 16, Paul gives the exhortation we all need to practice with one another regardless of which doctrines we promote:

> "But speaking the truth in love, may grow up into Him in all things, which is the Head, even Christ: From whom the whole body fitly joined together and compacted by that which every joint supplieth, according to the effectual working in the measure of every part, maketh increase of the body unto the edifying of itself in love."

When we understand fully that His shed blood alone brings us "nigh unto God", we may also realize the warning the Lord gave us in Revelation 2:4-5. Jesus said, "Nevertheless I have somewhat against thee, because thou hast left thy first love. Remember therefore from whence thou art fallen and repent and do the *first works* or else I will come unto thee quickly and will remove thy candlestick out of his place except thou repent." There can be no first works except the work that worked first: the blood of Jesus Christ, not our preferred doctrines, no matter how correct and scriptural they are. His blood is the bedrock of Christian faith and fellowship. All other doctrines fall in line behind His blood atonement.

9

Carrying Precious Spices

O ur natural inclination is to worry how we will do something, if things will come together at the right time, or if someone else on whom we depend will carry his, or her, share of the load. More often than not, the deed is done, the parts fit, and the people come through. But, if things don't work out, the sun still rises on the morrow and we draw our next breath.

In Mark 16:1-4, the women brought sweet spices to the tomb to anoint the body of Jesus. They left home at the rising of the sun worrying among themselves in verse three about the large stone at the entrance to His tomb. "Who shall roll us away the stone from the door of the sepulchre?" they said in verse 3. Yet, when they arrived and looked, the stone *was already rolled away.* Their worry had been for nothing.

What is so wonderful about this event for me, however, is these dear ladies knew the stone that barred their entry into the tomb was great. They knew they could not move it themselves, but they took their precious spices and went there anyway. How the Lord must have loved that! No wonder the stone was moved away upon their arrival! Love for Jesus carried them on their journey in spite of the difficulty they knew lay ahead. Duty and obligation can't do that; only love can.

If your heart is burning in you with desire for Jesus, if you are "constrained by the love of Christ", (2 Corinthians 5:14), you may suddenly discover one day that your "stone" has been tilted, shifted from you to Him, being moved, rolled away, by the same power that turned the stone, barring entry into His tomb....resurrection! *Life! His life!*

The spices you bring to Him for His "body" are wonderful in His sight. They are sweet. They are precious. They are costly. He knows they have been extracted from your life through the fires of suffering, the wounds of heartache, the pangs of disappointment. These spices are still meant for the body of Christ today. The aroma is just as sweet to Jesus now as the spices the women brought to Him so long ago.

In Mark 14:3-9, scripture tells us another event concerning a woman with spices. This woman, believed to be Mary of Bethany, the sister of Lazarus whom Jesus raised from the dead, came to anoint Jesus "aforehand" for His burial. Some of the disciples, Judas, in particular, thought it a waste of money. Jesus, however, thought it such an act of love that He said in vs. 8 and 9, *"She hath done what she could. She is come aforehand to anoint my body to the burying. Verily I say unto you, Wherever this gospel shall be preached throughout the whole world, this also that she hath done shall be spoken of for a memorial of her."*

Jesus had been expounding to His followers what must happen to Him in Jerusalem. Mary apparently must have had some understanding about this or Jesus would not have said she was doing it for His burial. She seemed to be in the company of few who did so. She did what she could. She did what she could! Jesus took very careful notice that she did what she could. Isn't that wonderful? He knows. He knows when you do what you can, and it is a precious thing to Him, Friend.

Mary came to Jesus *before the cross* with her spices, and Mary came *after the cross* with spices. She took the spices knowing the stone was great and she and the other ladies could not move it, but they took the spices anyway. They did what they could! They went with what was precious. They did what they could do, and Jesus took care of what they could not do. Praise Him forever!

10

Castaway

In Luke 9:22-27, Jesus is explaining to His disciples, as He often did, what will happen to Him, Son of Man, when they arrive in Jerusalem. He said that He must suffer, be rejected, slain, and then rise again on the third day. Then He explained to them the corresponding course, the opportunity, for those who would follow after Him.

In verse 23, He clearly states the road offered: "If *any man* will come after Me, let him deny himself, take up his cross and follow Me." All believers have a cross and Jesus is in front, with us following behind. Jesus goes on to say that losing our life is indeed how we save our life.

In verse 25, Jesus says two things can happen if a person does not follow this directive to live the cross life: "For what is a man advantaged if he gain the whole world and (1) lose himself or (2) be cast away."

The first (lose himself) can only mean the final separation from God that comes at the horrible second death when a man has refused the redemptive, precious blood of the Lamb. The second (cast away), however, brings to mind what the apostle Paul said in 1 Corinthians

9:27: "But I keep under my body and bring it into subjection lest that by any means when I should have preached to others, I myself should be a castaway." Paul kept his body in subjection to the spirit.

How sad indeed to become "shipwrecked" like Hymenaeus and Alexander, whom Paul described in 1 Timothy 1:18-20 where he said speaking to Timothy:

> "This charge I commit unto thee, son Timothy, according to the prophecies which went before on thee, that thou by them mightest war a good warfare; Holding faith, and a good conscience; which some having put away concerning faith have made shipwreck: Of whom is Hymenaeus and Alexander; whom I have delivered unto Satan, that they may learn not to blaspheme."

How sad indeed to become like Demas, a lover of this present world. Paul speaks of him in 2 Timothy 4:10: "For Demas hath forsaken me, having loved this present world, and is departed unto Thessalonica ...."

How sad indeed, like Judas, after having been closely associated with Jesus, day in and day out, seeing the miracles, hearing the word of the Lord, to in the end, betray Him with a kiss (Luke 22:47-48).

How sad like Ananias and Sapphira, having been present in the early church, experiencing the great grace and presence of the Holy Spirit, to be carried out dead for their attempted deception (Acts 5:1-11).

How sad indeed to be set aside as a dishonored vessel in the great house of the Lord. 2 Timothy 2:20-21 speaks of this:

> "But in a great house there are not only vessels of gold and of silver, but also of wood and of earth; and some to honour,

and some to dishonour. If a man therefore purge himself from these, he shall be a vessel unto honour, sanctified, and meet for the Master's use, and prepared unto every good work."

How sad, how terribly, horridly sad, to fall into the group who crucify the Lord afresh and put Him to open shame as described in Hebrew 6:4-6:

> "For it is impossible for those who were once enlightened, and have tasted of the heavenly gift, and were made partakers of the Holy Ghost, And have tasted the good word of God, and the powers of the world to come, If they fall away, to renew them again unto repentance; seeing they crucify to themselves the Son of God afresh and put Him to an open shame."

First Corinthians 10:11-12 tells us that things are written as examples for us: "Now all these things happened for examples: and they are written for our admonition, upon whom the ends of the world are come. Wherefore let him that thinketh he standeth take heed lest he fall."

Understanding the ease at which our flesh can lead us astray, we should have a greater realization of why the cross life is necessary. If we are yielded to the Lord, committed to following Him, with love He will arrange our environment providing just the right amount of fire, pressure, and grace to produce a vessel unto honor in His great house.

11

Constraints on Jesus

Scripture tells us the Lord Jesus gave up His position in heaven to come to us, to offer Himself as a spotless lamb for us. In Philippians 2:5-8, Paul describes this amazing transition from eternal power to human limitation by saying:

> "Let this mind be in you, which was also in Christ Jesus: Who, being in the form of God, thought it not robbery to be equal with God: But made Himself of no reputation, and took upon Him the form of a servant, and was made in the likeness of men: And being found in fashion as a man, He humbled Himself, and became obedient unto death, even the death of the cross."

Think about that. The eternal God willingly placed Himself in a position to experience death, not just any death, but the death of the cross.....cruel, painful, tortuous, humiliating, public death, surrounded by sneering soldiers, screeching demons, clueless disciples, and an absent Father. Incredible.

Think of the determination, the mental, emotional tenacity to *remain on* that cross when you had at your disposal all the forces of heaven to change your position at any moment. He "did not accept deliverance that (He) might obtain a better resurrection" (Hebrews 11:35). "Looking unto Jesus the author and finisher of our faith; who for the *joy that was set before Him endured the cross,* despising the shame, and is set down at the right hand of the throne of God" (Hebrews 12:2).

What a man! What a God! What a Saviour! What a plan to bruise your own son (Isaiah 53:10), that we sorry, full-of-corruption humans, could be changed from glory to glory and swing through those gates of pearl, caught up in His magnificent train! Hallelujah!

Have you ever thought that Jesus not only accepted the constraints of a human body, but He also accepted the constraints of the time and history into which He was born?

Think of the weary, hot travel, walking on dusty roads when He knew in His eternal mind about air-conditioned cars, jets, tennis shoes, and showers! He knew everything there was to know about microphones, stadiums, television, and the Internet when He shouted to be heard on hillsides by gathering crowds.

Remember when He told His disciples before the crucifixion that He had much to say to them but they were not able to bear it yet (John 16:12)? Think about all that He carried within Himself, as He knows the end from the beginning, the Alpha and the Omega, all the history, inventions, future events, the coming accomplishments and developments, everything we could ever ask or think about the coming kingdom age. He knows. He knew it then!

Can we "lend an ear" and say to Him, "Lord, tell us just a little more?" Are we in a heart position with Him, to "bear" the receiving of some of His glorious truths? We certainly know there are such things, for Paul went to the third heaven and "heard unspeakable words which it is not lawful for a man to utter" (2 Corinthians 12:4).

In 1 Corinthians 2:9, Paul quoted the scripture found in Isaiah 64:4, which says, "Eye hath not seen nor ear heard, neither have entered into the heart of man, the things which God hath prepared for them that love Him." Most people stop that scripture right there. However, Paul forges ahead in verse 10 of 1 Corinthians 2 with this: *But God hath revealed them unto us by His spirit*, for the Spirit searcheth all things, yea, the deep things of God." Glory be! He wants us to understand more about Himself and the coming kingdom age! There are deeper things. There is a going on in Christ.

Paul speaks of this "going on" in Hebrews 6:1-3, when he says:

> "Therefore, leaving the principles of the doctrine of Christ, *let us go on unto perfection*; not laying again the foundation of repentance from dead works, and of faith toward God, Of the doctrine of baptisms, and of laying on of hands, and of resurrection of the dead, and of eternal judgment. And *this we will do, if God permit*."

Paul wonderfully expresses this again in Ephesians 3:8-12, where he says:

> "Unto me, who am less than the least of all saints, is this grace given, that I should preach among the Gentiles the *unsearchable riches of Christ;* and to make all men see what is the fellowship of the mystery, which from the beginning of the world hath been hid in God, who created all things by Jesus Christ: to the intent that *now* unto the principalities and powers in heavenly places, *might be known by the church the manifold wisdom of God*, according to the eternal purpose which He purposed in Christ Jesus our Lord."

Jesus accepted the constraints of flesh, time, and history in order to bring us out of flesh, time, and history into the glorious revelation of Himself and the kingdom age to come. The question now is, "Are we listening?" Are we even in a position to hear what the Spirit is saying to the church? If we are intent on power or position, if we desire a crowd or a following hanging on our every word, if we long to be greater than our brothers or sisters, or want to call fire down on those who disagree, if we want to sit on His right or left, and consider ourselves important, then we still remain in the shallows.

Oh, God, help us to "launch out" into the deep where there is nothing under our feet but one Rock and we, satisfied as nameless, shall be found in Him.

12

Being Delivered

In Mark 9:31, Jesus told His disciples again what was going to happen to Him. He said He would be *delivered* into the hands of men and they would kill Him and He would rise on the third day.

Jesus was both Son of Man and Son of God. This dual existence was, and still is, the crux of everything eternal. The age-old question that Jesus asked is still relevant today: "Whom say *ye* that I am?" (Matthew 16:15). If you believe Jesus was just a man, that is one thing; but if you also believe that He was, and is, the Son of God, that is another thing and it requires a response.

Again in Mark 9:31, Jesus said that He, the Son of Man, *is delivered* into the hands of men. His captors did not take Him; He was delivered over to them by the determined will of God. It was, after all, the plan.

The Son of God, however, was *not* delivered unto the hands of men; He went along willingly. At any moment during that time and afterward, He could have simply "passed through the midst of them and gone His way" as He did in Luke 4:28-30.

Jesus could have called for legions of angels to come to His rescue, as He said in Matthew 26:53. "Thinkest thou that I cannot now pray to my Father and He shall presently give Me more than twelve legions of angels?" Son of Man was *delivered over* to the crowd, but Son of God purposely went with them. What a difference!

When Jesus stood before Pilate, having been physically delivered to him as Son of Man, Pilate told Jesus that he had the power to release Him. Jesus responded by saying, "Thou couldest have no power *at all* against Me, except it were given thee from above: therefore he that delivered Me unto thee hath the greater sin" (John 19:11).

Son of Man was at the mercy of His "delivered circumstances" but Son of God, *never*. The Son of God submitted to the weakness present in His human body. In that weakness, yielded quietly to the Father's powerful plan, lay the strength of the very one who created all things as we are told in Colossians 1:16. "For *by Him* were all things created, that are in heaven, and that are in earth, visible and invisible, whether they be thrones, or dominions, or principalities, or powers: all things were created by Him and for Him."

Should not this realization keep us forever on our faces as we contemplate what was done for us by this God-man?

13

Be Not Afraid but Speak

Even for joyful Christians, frustration and discouragement can creep, or leap, into our lives on occasion. Our natural man just gravitates that way when we spend ourselves and see no immediate results, or appreciation for our work.

In Acts 18, Paul came to Corinth, where he stayed with Aquila and Priscilla. While there, verse 4 tells us he reasoned in the synagogue every Sabbath and persuaded the Jews and the Greeks.

In verse 5, Silas and Timothy came from Macedonia, and Paul felt pressed in the spirit to testify to the Jews that Jesus was the Christ. However, for all his speaking and preaching, the Jews opposed themselves and blasphemed. Paul's reaction to this was strong. He shook his raiment and replied to them, "Your blood be upon your own heads. I am clean. From henceforth I will go unto the Gentiles." Paul was through with the Jews! But Jesus wasn't, not yet, not in Corinth. He was about to save the chief ruler of the synagogue!

Paul departed into the house of Justus (v.7), whose house just happened to join the synagogue. In the very next verse (8), we are told that Crispus, the chief ruler of the synagogue, believed on the

Lord with all his house and many of the Corinthians, hearing, believed and were baptized!

Remembering how Paul had stood against the Lord at the first, hauling believers to jail, and holding the coats of those who killed Stephen, we might think he would have been more understanding of the Jews' refusal to believe Jesus to be the promised Messiah. It is so easy to be discouraged when you meet with a blank stare or a hardened heart.

In verses 9 and 10, we are told that the Lord spoke to Paul in the night by a vision, saying, *"Be not afraid, but speak* and hold not thy peace for I *am with thee,* and no man shall set on thee to hurt thee for I have much people in this city."* What a word of encouragement for the discouraged and apparently fearful Paul!

What a word of encouragement for us as well. We too can gather much from the Lord's word to Paul in verses 9 and 10. Don't be afraid. Speak. He is with you. He is aware of where you are and the people around you.

So, after shaking his garment and declaring himself through with the Jews in Corinth, verse 11 tells us that Paul "continued there, a year and six months, teaching the word of God among them." Verse 19 also tells us that in Ephesus, Paul entered the synagogue and reasoned with the Jews.

Circumstances and the reactions of others may convince us that it's time to give up on someone or something, and we may be completely justified in doing so. That is when we need to remember this episode in the life of Paul and speak on, pray on, walk on, and press on in the faith. We never know when the Lord may come into a situation and change lives all around us because we spoke on.

Galatians 6:9-10 tells us, "Don't be weary in well doing for in due season we shall reap, if we faint not. As we have therefore opportunity, let us do good unto all men, especially unto them who are of the household of faith." Amen.

14

Draw Me and We Will Run

I n the Song of Solomon there is a lovely scripture found in chapter 1:4, which reads, "Draw *me, we* will run after thee. The King hath brought me into His chambers. *We* will be glad and rejoice in Thee. We will remember Thy love more than wine. The upright love Thee."

This scripture does not say, "Draw me and I will run." No, it states, "Draw me and we will run." The King brings me into His chambers, and we, not just me, shall rejoice.

What a wonderful truth! If I am drawn to Christ and respond accordingly, there will be a corresponding movement toward Jesus in the lives of others. If the King brings me into His chambers, then I am in a close and more personal place of awareness of Him, which will influence others to be in that same place.

In the King's chambers, there is intimacy ... closeness ... worship. It seems almost a sacrilege to speak of such a place, yet Jesus is a very personal Saviour. He desires us to know Him as we are known by Him. He desires us to "grow up into Him in all things, which is the head, even Christ" (Ephesians 4:15).

Jesus desires each to not only be a worshiper, but a friend. He desires for His followers to know Him for Himself, not just to want His power, or His blessings, no matter how wonderful they are.

If you abide in the vine with such closeness, you cannot help but draw others to Him as well. Your very "manner of life" (2 Timothy 3:10) will draw them to run after Him too.

Remember, "The King hath brought me into His chambers. *We* will be glad and rejoice in Thee. *We* will remember Thy love more than wine. The upright love Thee " (Song of Solomon 1:4).

In John 4:23-24, Jesus Himself said:

> "But the hour cometh, and *now is*, when the *true worshippers shall* worship the Father in spirit and in truth: for the Father seeketh such to worship Him. God is a Spirit: and they that worship Him *must* worship Him in spirit and in truth."

If you are worshiping Him in spirit and in truth, your life cannot help but draw others to Christ. This is the manner of life that compels others to ask you about the reason for the hope they see in you (1 Peter 3:15). This is the manner of life that causes others to report, "that God is in you of a truth."

Oh, to live in the King's chambers! Draw *me* and we will run!

15

Ears to Hear ... What a Blessing!

When asked by a scribe which was the first commandment of all, Jesus responded in Mark 12:29 with the following statement, "The first of all the commandments is, 'Hear, O Israel; The Lord our God is one Lord.'" Hear...Hear...Hear.

After first directing them to hear, then Jesus instructs how to obey that first commandment when He said in verse 30, "And thou shalt love the Lord thy God with all thy heart and with all thy soul, and with all thy mind and all thy strength, this is the first commandment."

Then adding the second commandment in verse 31, Jesus said, "And the second is like, namely this, Thou shalt love thy neighbor as thyself. There is none other commandment greater than these."

In reading Mark 4:23-25, Jesus spoke again of "ears to hear":

> "If any man have *ears to hear*, let him hear. And He said unto them. 'Take heed what ye hear, with what measure ye mete, (distribute) it shall be measured to you: and unto you that hear shall more be given. For he that hath, to him shall be

given: and he that hath not, from him shall be taken even that which he hath.'"

How can something be taken away from a person if he never had it? As long as a person lives on this earth, the opportunity to accept Christ as Saviour is ever present, but the moment death comes, his fate is sealed one way or the other. The opportunity is taken away. He loses what he once had ... the chance to know Christ in this life as well as in the life to come. Oh, how important to hear and then respond in the affirmative.

It is a great blessing to have "ears that hear" what the Spirit is saying to the church today. It is also a great responsibility, for the Lord expects divinely led distribution of what He has spoken. Freely we receive, and freely we should give.

Remember that in Mark 4:24 Jesus said, "What measure ye mete, (distribute) it shall be measured to you and unto you that hear shall more be given." Some people read this, and, sadly, their hearts only think of money and worldly gain. Oh, but it is so *much more* than that!

Once your "ears" are opened to the Lord and His scriptures, as you read and obey what you understand, then, as you continue on in the Lord, more and more will follow.

God will *never* speak anything contrary to scripture. Never. He can and will, however, enlighten our understanding of scripture. When a man thinks he knows something, he knows nothing as he ought (1 Corinthians 8:2). There is *always* room for further understanding and enlargement. The Holy Spirit will speak, affirming the things that concern Jesus.

It is a wonderful experience to hear God through His scriptures. When the Holy Spirit speaks of Jesus through the written word, it becomes the Living Word, which enlarges and expands our understanding of the Lord Himself. We grow in grace and in the knowledge of the truth. What a wonderful thing to have "ears to hear"!

Jesus said in verse 24 to "take heed what you hear". Be sure what you hear and read is scriptural. If you are a book reader, read the works of Christian authors who finished well and whose ministries are Christ-centered.

Read the scripture, especially the New Testament, over and over. Begin in Matthew and read through Revelation, and then start over again. Never stop. You don't have to try to memorize scripture; the Holy Spirit will "bring scripture to your remembrance " as you need it (John 14:26). Try to read at least three or four chapters at a time. Read slowly with expectation. You may read for some time before your "ears" begin to hear, but they will begin to hear for Jesus still has "much to say" (John 16:12).

Don't think of "revelation" as some spooky, ethereal thing, or always a prediction about the future. Revelation is an understanding about the Lord Jesus that you previously did not know. This understanding always existed. You just did not realize it.

Many times we hear the scripture in 1 Corinthians 2:9 quoted with a tone of great, solemn mystery. In verse 9 Paul said, "But as it is written, 'Eye hath not seen, nor ear heard, neither have entered into the heart of man, the things which God hath prepared for them that love Him.' " They speak this scripture as though we will never understand anything more until we depart to the next life.

Paul, however, after writing that scripture, which is a quote from the Old Testament of Isaiah 64:4, gives us the New Testament glorious response by saying in 1 Corinthians 2:10-13:

"But God *hath revealed them unto us by His Spirit:* for the Spirit searcheth all things, yea, the deep things of God. For what man knoweth the things of a man, save the spirit of man which is in him? even so the things of God knoweth no man, but the Spirit of God. Now we have received, not the spirit of the world, but the spirit which is of God; that *we might know the things that are freely given to us of God.* Which things also we speak, not in the words which man's wisdom teacheth, but which the *Holy Spirit teacheth*; comparing spiritual things with spiritual."

Revelation can be a word, or a thought, that acts as a catalyst leading you to more and more understanding--always Godward and upward, helping you to "...grow up into Him in all things which is the Head, even Christ" (Ephesians 4:15).

One scripture will connect with another, then another, all coming to you as the picture of understanding is enlarged in your heart first, then in your mind, thus giving you words to speak what you have "heard" in the spirit.

You cannot force revelation. Your part is to ask for "ears to hear" what the Spirit is saying to the church (Revelation 2:29). If your heart's desire is to truly follow on to know the Lord, if you long after Him whether it mean prosperity or poverty, if you desire Him above the praise of men or the exaltation of self, you will have "ears to hear".

God does not operate by contrived formulas, however noble sounding or scripturally inspired. He is a heart-monitoring God. You cannot fool Him. He knows what desires rest in your heart. The "good ground" lies like a fertile field waiting for the entrance of the seed and the production of fruit. He actively seeks after those who will worship Him in Spirit and in truth, who long in their hearts to hear what He has to say.

16

Finding Brethren

S ometimes, I have wondered why Jesus often took Peter, James, and John apart from His other disciples. Those three were with Jesus in some very special moments. They were with Him on the mount of transfiguration seeing His glory. There seemed to be a special bond between these three, yet we know Jesus was, and is, no respecter of persons (Acts 10:34). His love and "being accepted in the beloved" is extended to one and all who receive Him as Lord and Saviour (Ephesians 1:6).

In Acts 28, we read details of Paul's sea mishap on his voyage to Rome as a prisoner. Something wonderful happened to Paul and those traveling with him to Rome. It was in a little coastal town called Puteoli in Italy. Not much has been said about this event, but it has heartwarming implications.

Acts 28:13-14 reads:

> "And from thence we fetched a compass, and came to Rhegium: and after one day the south wind blew, and we came the next day to Puteoli: Where *we found brethren,* and

were desired to tarry (invited to stay) with them seven days: and so we went to Rome."

What a wonderful thing it must have been after such a perilous ocean voyage full of horrific storms, scared sailors, long fasting, fervent prayer, shipwreck, floating to shore on boards and planks, being bitten by a viper, to suddenly, in a little coastal town ... *find brethren*!

Yes, Paul found brethren. These brethren didn't just give a hug and bid them well, but they desired them to tarry with them for seven days, eating, resting, recovering, refreshing, and being refreshed in the Lord. What a wonderful encounter that must have been! How like the Lord to guide even a sinking ship full of hard-headed sailors who refused to heed Paul's warning in the first place, to guide them all with no loss of life to this particular little town where Paul found brethren.

17

Forward on Their Journey

There are some verses of scripture found in 3 John that you seldom hear quoted, but they are full of meaning and encouragement for us all. John is writing a letter to Gaius, a well-beloved brother in the faith.

In verse 4, John says he has no greater joy than to know that his children, those whom he has personally brought up and nourished in the Lord, are walking in truth. He speaks in verse 5 that one way he knows they are walking in truth is their treatment of the brethren and strangers.

In verse 6, John speaks this witness of others by saying, "Which have borne witness of thy charity before the church: whom if thou *bring forward on their journey* after a godly sort, thou shalt do well." Forward ... on their journey ... after a godly sort. How important is that! Forward! Godly sort! No going backward, only forward! Only godly! We are all on a journey. How important it is as we meet others along this "way" that we offer encouragement that helps move them "forward".

This reminds me of the V-shaped flocks of migrating birds. The bird at the point of the V breaks the wind pressure, which makes flying easier for those following behind. The lead bird tires more easily. Those experiencing the benefit of less wind pressure at the sides of the V call to the one in front encouraging him as he uses his energy to help them. When the lead bird tires, he falls back into the line, and another moves forward to take his place. We all need encouragement. Sometimes we lead. Sometimes we follow. Even those who are greatest in faith among us may grow weary along their journey and be encouraged by others to continue as the apostle Paul was by the coming of Titus.

I remember an old saint saying once that the ditch runs beside the road. If you fall in the ditch, don't stay in the ditch. If you mess up, get up! Get back on the road. Get back on your journey. How important it is to reach your hand to a brother or sister who may have fallen in the ditch and help them up; help them forward on their journey again after a godly sort.

> "Now we exhort you, brethren, warn them that are unruly, comfort the feebleminded, support the weak, be patient towards all men. See that none render evil for evil unto any man; but ever follow that which is good, both among yourselves, and to all men" (1 Thessalonians 5:14-15).

If you live long enough, you may be the one who is feebleminded or weak. You may be the one needing the word of encouragement, or a hand up out of the ditch. We can never go wrong by encouraging all to go "forward on their journey after a godly sort".

18

From That Time Forth

In Matthew 16:13-28, Jesus asked His disciples two very important questions, "Who do men say that I, the Son of Man, am?" and, "Whom say ye that I am?"

We know, of course, that Peter answered the questions with revelation given by the Father in heaven when he said, "Thou art the Christ, the Son of the living God."

Jesus responded to Peter's answer by replying in verses 17-19:

> "And Jesus answered and said unto him, 'Blessed art thou, Simon Bar-jona: for flesh and blood hath not revealed it unto thee, but My Father in heaven. And I say also unto thee, That thou art Peter, and upon this rock (this revelation) I will build My church; and the gates of hell shall not prevail against it. And I will give unto thee (My church) the keys of the kingdom of heaven: and whatsoever thou shalt bind on earth shall be bound in heaven: and whatsoever thou shalt loose on earth shall be loosed in heaven.'"

The revelation that Jesus is both Son of Man and Son of God, is the cornerstone, not only upon which the church is built, but also upon which we are personally "built". Hell can assail, but never prevail, over the church, or the individual, who has been given this revelation of Jesus Christ. Knowing this in your depths as a church, or an individual, gives access to the power of God to bind or loose, but only at the discretion of the Lord. Herein lies the power of the righteous man to avail much in fervent prayer (James 5:16).

Now that Jesus has expounded unto them this revelation about Himself, He proceeds to tell them an astounding series of events, which are about to happen to Him, even though He is *both* Son of Man and Son of God.

In Matthew 16:21, comes the catch phrase, "*From that time forth* began Jesus to shew unto His disciples how that He *must* go unto Jerusalem and suffer many things of the elders and chief priests and scribes, and be killed, and be raised again the third day."

How this next information must have been like a pop to their balloon after just hearing about power to bind and loose in heaven! No wonder Peter thought these things could not possibly happen to Jesus. He was God as well as man! Peter's concept of authority did not include suffering as a descriptive element.

Seeing Jesus as Son of God, really *seeing* Him as Son of God, is knowing in your depths that He is *sovereign Lord* and *Christ*! And *from that time forth*, you know He is sovereign over the events in your life no matter how perplexing, distressing, or inexplicably difficult they may be.

From that time forth (until you *know* He is sovereign Son of God), you limit what He can show you and speak to you about His life in you and what He wishes to do with His life in you. Until you know Him as sovereign in your life, neither will you be able to understand what scripture means in Philippians 3:10, which speaks of fellowshipping with His sufferings, being made conformable unto His death. No, we prefer the power to bind and loose. This is a better fit to the natural man who wants to rule and reign over someone or something.

True authority does not lie in quoting scripture vigorously and attempting to bind the enemy. True authority lies in submission to Him as Son of God, sovereign Lord and Christ and following Him, not your own inclinations of what a perfect world should look like.

James 4:6-7 speaks to us concerning the pipeline through which the authority of God flows:

> "But He giveth more grace. Wherefore He saith, 'God resisteth the proud, but giveth grace unto the humble.' *Submit yourselves therefore to God.* Resist the devil, and he will flee from you."

Power lies in submission to sovereign God. Someone once said that Jesus took the cup, not because of the cup or what was in the cup, but because of the hand that held the cup out to Him. He understood the sovereignty of Father God. Once we really believe that as well, there is a great power shift and a going forth in our lives.

19

Fruit to Perfection

J esus gives the parable of the sower in Luke 8:5-15. In verse 14, He says, "And that which fell among thorns are they, which when they have heard, go forth, and are choked with cares and riches and pleasures of this life, and bring no *fruit to perfection.*" It wasn't that the tree had no fruit. It was that the fruit was halted in the ripening process and left short of perfection. Ever try to eat green fruit? It is sour, hard, and bitter. It pains the belly if consumed.

The blossom that drew attention to itself at the first is long gone. The processing of time, sun, rain, and, most importantly, life-giving sap from the tree, all have worked together for the good of the fruit. The ripening has happened over time, and the fruit is now ready for consumption. The Lord gathers the fruit, blesses it, opens it, and gives it to others at the peak of ripeness.

We would think this would be the "fruit to perfection", when our lives at last are given as fruit to nourish and help sustain others. Yet, there is another step in the processing of fruit unto perfection.

In Isaiah 53:10, scripture says, "Yet it pleased the Lord to bruise Him; He hath put Him (Jesus) to grief: when thou shalt make His soul an offering for sin, He shall *see His seed*, He shall prolong His days, and the pleasure of the Lord shall prosper in His hand."

The final stage of perfect fruit ... He shall see His seed. The blossom stage of being known and esteemed of men, the consumption stage of being broken and poured out for others, now leads to a precious seed...a life lost to self. He alone knows the true value of this seed, for He alone knows all the years of processing that have brought the seed to this point: the winds, the storms, the hot sun, the droughts, the attacks of outside forces, the tender hands of the vinedresser. All have worked to bring forth the moment when the Lord sees His seed in a life that has become one with Him and with the Father. "I in them and thou in Me that they may be made perfect in one..."(John 17:23). This is the seed that has fallen into the ground and died to itself bringing forth the true likeness of the Saviour. He sees Himself in this life. Paul labored again until Christ was *formed*, not just born, in believers (Galatians 4:19). This is fruit unto perfection for it now produces "fruit after its kind."

20

God's Timing in a Fish

S o often we grow uncomfortable with our perception of God's timing in our life's events. We wait for God to move, and meanwhile, we stew. We feel better for a while; then more time passes, and we wonder and wander and stew some more.

In Matthew 17:25-27, there is a wonderful lesson illustrating the timing, patience, and provision of God. This scripture gives us the only incident in which Jesus performed a miracle for Himself, actually half for Himself. It is the miracle of one fish that just happened to have a coin in its mouth.

Jesus and Peter had been discussing tribute money given to kings. In verse 27, Jesus said to Peter, "Notwithstanding, lest we should offend them, go thou to the sea, and cast an hook, and take up the fish that first cometh up; and when thou has opened his mouth, thou shalt find a piece of money: that take, and give unto them *for Me and thee.*"

Jesus gave Peter such specific instructions. We just read over this and move on to chapter 18, tucking this event in the rear of the miracle list. Have you ever considered this fish and that piece of money in its mouth? What a lesson!

I wonder about that piece of money. How long had it been in the sea? Where did it come from? Perhaps a fisherman lost it from his pocket while casting a net. Maybe a young child threw it in the water, or a boat overturned, spilling its contents into the sea.

One thing for sure, Jesus knew about that one piece of money the same as He knows when a single sparrow falls to the ground. It's hard for us to comprehend a mind that can be aware simultaneously of all the events in the universe as well as all the thoughts and actions of every man, woman, child, and fish!

Yes, there is that fish. That one fish that the Lord was so specific about. He told Peter to take the first fish he caught and look in its mouth. Millions of fish swam in the sea of Galilee, but this one fish saw that one coin and scooped it up, holding it in its mouth! Not only did this one fish pick up this one coin; he did not swallow the coin. He held it in his mouth. Now, it had to swim by Peter's hook and bite it! Yes, Peter had to be standing in the right place at the exact moment for this particular fish to swim by his hook and take the hook before any other fish did. Remember, it had to be the first fish.

Think about that. Think about the absolute preparation and timing of this one episode. How amazing is this whole sequence of events! No wonder we are told as Christians to be "anxious for nothing but in every thing by prayer and supplication with thanksgiving let your requests be made known unto God" (Philippians 4:6).

Sovereign God, who can take care of such details as the placement of coin, fish, Peter, and his hook, can be trusted to guide you and me through the confusing maze that sometimes overwhelms our lives.

It's amazing to me that there is no record given of Peter's response to this miracle. However, Jesus also wondered why they did not understand the multiplication of the loaves and fishes (Matthew 16:9). So often, we humans are just so slow, so very slow to get it. Good grief!

21

Hearing and Seeing

T he hearing ear and the seeing eye, the Lord hath made even both of them (Proverbs 20:12).

If you are born again by the Spirit of the Living God, you heard something. Someone preached the gospel, the good news of Jesus Christ. Someone shared words from the written word about the Living Word, and you heard it. You heard the word and you saw your sin. You saw your need for a Saviour. You saw that Jesus Christ was indeed the Son of God. You heard and saw the *way,* the *truth,* and the *life* of salvation. You repented of your sins. You received the precious blood of the Lamb on the doorpost of your heart. Your name was written in the Lamb's Book of Life, accompanied by the rejoicing of angels. You were accepted in the beloved and inserted into the family of God. Wow! That's a lot to hear and see!

Whether your salvation experience began as a tender child trusting Jesus with wide-eyed wonder, as an adult kneeling in hot tears of shame, or somewhere in between, you heard, you saw, and you received. You began your journey.

In Luke 10:23-24 Jesus said:

> "Blessed are the eyes which see the things that ye see: For I tell you, that many prophets and kings have desired to see those things which ye see, and have not seen them; and to hear those things which ye hear, and have not heard them."

In Matthew 13:16-17 the same account reads:

> "But blessed are your eyes, for they see: and your ears, for they hear. For verily I say unto you, That many prophets and righteous men have desired to see those things which ye see, and have not seen them; and to hear those things which ye hear, and have not heard them."

Never take for granted your "seeing eyes" and "hearing ears". Many, many throughout the ages longed for what you have, and went by way of the grave having never experienced His life. Do not neglect so great a salvation!

22

Prisons and Prisoners

J ohn the Baptist recognized Jesus as the Christ of God. He did this at the baptism of Jesus when he proclaimed Him as the Lamb of God who takes away the sins of the world. John pointed out to his followers that Jesus must increase and he, John, would decrease. However, John finds himself imprisoned because he dared to speak against the marriage of Antipas to Philip's wife, Herodias, who was his own niece. Prisons, of one type or another, can cause a lot of distress.

In prison John hears about the works of Jesus. He sends two of his own disciples to ask Jesus a question, "Art thou He that should come, or do we look for another?" (Matthew 11:2-6). What a strange question to ask of the one you have publicly declared to be the Christ of God!

Jesus's reply sent back to John is gripping. In Matthew 11:4-6 Jesus sends this response to John:

> "Go and show John *again* (Has He had to do this before?) those things which ye do hear and see: The blind receive their sight, and the lame walk, the lepers are cleansed, and

the deaf hear, the dead are raised up, and the poor have the gospel preached to them."

Then Jesus adds a pointed observation that I am sure struck the heart of John. He said, "And blessed is he whosoever shall not be offended in Me."

One can only assume that the bars that closed around John had succeeded in bringing him to a place of doubt about Jesus as the promised Messiah.

The sovereignty of God allowed the greatest born of women (Matthew 11:11) to remain imprisoned, and he was seemingly offended. The last of the old covenant prophets was murdered as the new covenant King was beginning His ministry.

Jesus said John was the greatest born of women ... the natural birth ... then declared the spiritual birth superior by adding, "notwithstanding he that is least in the kingdom of Heaven is greater than he" (Matthew 11:11). The New Covenant is superior to the old!

In Matthew 11:12, Jesus further says, "And from the days of John the Baptist *until now* the Kingdom of Heaven suffereth violence, and the violent take it by force." *Until now* ... the old was still in effect, but that was about to change and soon. Heaven would suffer just one more act of violence. That last act would end violence forever in heaven's domain. There would remain no more sacrifice for sin. The Lord provided *Himself as* the Lamb! Prisoners were about to be released from their cells!

23

Other Prisons and Prisoners

In Acts 12:5-19, scripture tells us of Peter's prison experience. King Herod imprisoned Peter because doing so pleased the Jews. Sixteen soldiers guarded Peter. It would not have mattered if a thousand had guarded him. Prayer was being made without ceasing for Peter. God moved sovereignly, sending an angel to wake Peter up. Peter was sleeping like a baby with apparently no offense as John the Baptist had experienced.

Peter was so content he thought his escape was all a vision until, suddenly, he came to himself outside the prison, a free man! The dear saints didn't even believe it when Peter showed up where they were praying, knocking at the door. (I always felt kind of sorry for the poor soldiers who slept through Peter's escape, losing their lives as a result. They were clueless!)

Next, we have the imprisonment of Paul and Silas in Acts 16:22-33. Paul and Silas were certainly not offended because of their prison time. They sang praises at midnight, and the other prisoners heard them. God must have also, because suddenly there was a great earthquake. All the prison doors opened, not just those of Paul and

Silas. Sometimes the benefits of God spill over into the lives of total strangers.

The prisoners' bands were all loosened. The jail keeper drew his sword to kill himself when Paul's voice came loudly crying out to him, "Do thyself no harm for we are *all* here." Imagine that, prisoners refusing to escape their prison. The same power that shook the locks off now gripped the jailed men. Revival was about to break out! Most of us would probably have fallen all over each other getting out, but they remained ... all of them.

The jailer fell down before Paul and Silas, asking, "Sirs, what must I do to be saved?" The scripture does not mention what happened to the other prisoners who also experienced the great release, but only tells us they remained. One can only surmise that they also received salvation as well, or they would surely have left.

"Blessed are those who are not offended in me," Jesus had told the imprisoned John the Baptist. Blessed are those who do not doubt His sovereignty when the bars close around them. Blessed are those who remain in difficult circumstances, demonstrating by their very manner of life praises to the great King. Psalm 40:3 says, "And He hath put a new song in my mouth, even praise unto our God: many shall *see it* and fear, and shall trust in the Lord."

Fancy that ... seeing a song! Oh, that our lives in difficulty would sing His praises and through their song would help initiate the freedom of many who all their lifetime have lived in bondage.

24

In Between Prisons

John the Baptist had been told "again" by Jesus in Matthew 11:4-5, via his disciples, all that was being done in the ministry of Jesus. Jesus added by explaining that blessing is upon those who are not offended in Him.

Jesus continues explaining in Matthew 11:14, that John was indeed Elias which was to come as the forerunner of His ministry by preparing His way explaining the need for repentance and water baptism.

In Matthew 14:12-13, John's disciples come to Jesus to tell Him of John's death. Jesus is so moved, He desires to depart by ship into a desert place to be alone. This was His plan, but the people changed that. A great multitude followed Him on foot out of the cities. He who had a plan for solitude was moved with compassion (v.14) toward them, and He healed the sick among them.

Jesus could flow with His circumstances. He was fluid in His walk. He could easily be put upon by the desperate circumstances of others. (Oh, to be more like Jesus!)

It is now evening in this desert place. The people are hungry. The disciples want to send the crowd away to find food as best they can, but wonderful Jesus says, "You give them to eat." But there are only five loaves and two fishes. However, little is much when God is in it! The key lies in the statement of Jesus, "Bring them hither to Me" (v.18). He demonstrates order by having the thousands sit on the grass. He blesses, He breaks, and He gives.

Now, finally, finally, Jesus constrains His disciples to get into a ship and go before Him to the other side while He sends the multitudes away. At last He goes up into a mountain apart to pray. Blessed alone! Blessed alone with the Father to talk privately about John the Baptist.

For John, He obviously sorrowed. For the martyr, Stephen, He will stand up by the throne of His glory to receive him in heaven! His position will have dramatically changed, and so will His response to death. Has our position changed, as well, concerning death?

Jesus would soon have the keys to hell and death on His key chain. The last martyr under the old covenant brought sorrow. The first martyr under the new covenant brought joy unspeakable and full of glory, for precious in the sight of the Lord is the death of His saints (Psalm 116:15). For John He sorrowed; for Stephen, He stood up rejoicing!

25

Is the Old Better?

A dear friend of mine is facing what many of us will as we age and can no longer live independently. While praying with her about the situation, the Holy Spirit opened a scripture to my heart. The scripture is found in John 19:26-27. Jesus was hanging on the cross dying for the sins of the world, yet in His great suffering, He made provision for Mary, His dear mother.

Those verses read:

> "When Jesus therefore saw His mother, and the disciple standing by, whom He loved, He saith unto His mother, 'Woman, behold thy son!' Then saith He to the disciple, 'Behold, thy mother!' And from that hour that disciple took her unto his own home."

Yes, what a blessed man, who, though He was God, considered the needs of His mother, not only making provision for her eternal soul, but also for that of her humanity.

Have we ever considered what a change this relocation would be for Mary? Mary was still a fairly young woman in her late forties or early fifties. Mark 6:3 tells us she had at least six children other than Jesus, who was around thirty-three when He went to the cross.

Mark 6:3 states, "Is not this the carpenter, the son of Mary, the brother of James, and Joses, and of Judah, and Simon? And are not His sisters here with us? And they were offended at Him."

Some of His siblings were surely married and had homes in which Mary could have lived, or may have been living already, since there is no mention of Joseph still being alive.

What about John? He had a home, or Jesus would not have sent Mary there. What about "Mrs." John? Would Mary also be bringing younger siblings of Jesus along with her?

As human beings, change is not always easy to accept. We often resist, or at least find it difficult, although we know it may be in our best interest. In Luke 5:39, Jesus said, "No man also having drunk old wine straightway desireth new for he saith, 'The old is better.'"

However, we remember that at the most excruciating moment of His earthly life, Jesus tenderly cared for His precious mother. He knew every detail of her existence, present and future. In His wisdom, He directed a huge change in her life even as He was dying.

Scripture does not record the emotional responses of Mary and John to this change. It does tell us that "from that hour", she went home with John. We know that the same sweet obedience that existed in Mary's heart when the angel Gabriel pronounced the coming birth of Jesus was still present. Her choice once again was, "Be it unto me according to Thy word" (Luke 1:38). Neither do we know the responses of Mary's other children to this new arrangement. We only know, it was so.

Jesus was loving His mother by orchestrating this move. As perplexing as it may have been to her, John, or others, He saw it simply as what needed to be done at that time with no explanation given or received. Amen.

26

Judging

In Matthew 7:1, we read the words of Jesus, which are some of the most quoted in scripture. "Judge not that ye be not judged." Most people stop there and don't follow through with the rest of the verses. Verse 5 tells us, "*First* cast out the beam out of thine own eye, and *then* shalt thou *see clearly* to cast out the mote out of thy brother's eye." We must be sure we are proceeding in righteousness before approaching another who is not.

Seldom will you hear quoted John 7:24. Jesus also said, "Judge not according to the appearance, but judge *righteous judgment*." So, how can Jesus tell us in Matthew 7:1, not to judge, then in John 7:24, He tells us to judge? Remember that all-important word that precedes "judgment" in John 7:24. That word is *"righteous"*.

What is righteous judgment? Righteous judgment is in agreement always with the spirit and intent of scripture. Always. Righteous judgment agrees with scripture in the Spirit of Jesus Christ. Unrighteous judgment comes with a condemning cruelty that has the threat of finality about it. Only God can give final judgment. We simply agree with His word and offer hope through the forgiveness of Jesus Christ.

In Luke 9:54-56, Jesus spoke expressly about the wrong kind of judgment. He had been refused lodging in a Samaritan village as they went towards Jerusalem. His disciples, James and John, were so livid about this that they wanted to "command fire to come down from heaven and consume them, even as Elias did." In verses 55-56, Jesus nailed unrighteous judgment when He said, "Ye know not what *manner of spirit ye are of.* For the Son of man is not come to destroy men's lives but to save them." There were still beams in the eyes of James and John, even though they had just been with Jesus on the mount of transfiguration! They wanted to issue permanent judgment, but only God can do that. In righteous judgment, forgiveness and hope are always presented first.

Righteous judgment does not desire to "bring fire down" on someone but rather longs to "lift up" out of sin and into a right relationship with God through Jesus Christ. Always. Nevertheless, righteous judgment always agrees with scripture and does not sugarcoat sin. In fact, righteous judgment is by its spiritual reality and oneness with scripture, "… sharper than any two-edged sword, piercing even to the dividing asunder of soul and spirit, and of the joints and marrow, and is a discerner of the thoughts and intents of the heart" (Hebrews 4:12).

Righteous judgment shines into the darkness, reveals; then in love, it covers the multitude of sins with the blood of Jesus (1Peter 4:8). It restores rather than destroys a person.

Always, always, as long as we live in this current world, our judgment should be redemptive, yet always in agreement with the spirit and intent of the scriptures. Only God Himself can pass final, eternal judgment as He alone is fully aware of the motive and intent of the heart.

God makes no error in His final judgment, for scripture declares in 2 Timothy 2:19: "Nevertheless the foundation of God standeth sure;

having this seal, *the Lord knoweth them that are His.* And, Let every one that nameth the name of Christ depart from iniquity."

Until God's final judgment, we as disciples of Christ should live our lives as salt and light in this present evil world. Doing that alone will make others aware of the motes in their own eyes. It cannot help but be so. By God's grace may we be able in love to help remove those motes and point the way to Christ.

27

Knowing What Is in Man

In John 2:23-25, Jesus was in Jerusalem with His disciples. Many believed in Him when they saw the miracles He did. However, in verses 24 and 25, scripture tells us, "But Jesus did not commit Himself unto them, because *He knew all men,* And needed not that any should testify of man: for *He knew what was in man.*"

Ephesians 5:8 speaks also to us concerning what is in man when it says, "For *ye were sometimes darkness, but now are ye light in the Lord*: walk as children of light."

We were not just "in darkness", we "were darkness". Jesus knew the darkness that was in man and came to transform it with His marvelous *light.*

True conversion comes via this revelation of self-darkness. All at once we "see" as Jesus does that we *are darkness* and need His light. This is the moment of intense personal conviction from the Holy Spirit. This is the moment when "the entrance of Thy word giveth light" (Psalm 119:130). This is the new birth experience. Until that event takes place, no matter what good deeds you do or what "church" you join, you are still darkness.

Jesus said in John 8:12, "I am the light of the world: He that followeth Me shall not walk in darkness, but shall have the light of life." When we receive the "Light of the World" (Jesus) into our hearts, we begin to really see things as they are, not how men have painted them to be, but how they really are.

When this transformation has taken place and we are born from above of His Spirit, the whole of our life should be taken up with the instruction given to us by John in 1 John 1:7: "But if we *walk in the light*, as He is in the light, we have fellowship one with another, and the blood of Jesus Christ His Son cleanseth us from all sin."

28

Knowledge of Salvation or Life?

In Luke 1:67-79, Zacharias, the Father of John the Baptist, was filled with the Holy Ghost and began to prophesy about his newborn son.

In verses 76 and 77, Zacharias said, " And thou, child, shall be called the prophet of the Highest: for thou shalt go before the face of the Lord to prepare His ways; To *give knowledge of salvation* unto His people by the remission of their sins ..."

John, of course, was the last of the old covenant prophets and the only one of them to actually see the "face" of the one about whom he prophesied ... the highest, the Lord of glory, Jesus Christ.

John could only give "knowledge of salvation". He could only demonstrate the channels through which the life would flow. It is not the channels that give life, however.

Romans 8:1-2 describes this Life in the channel by stating, "There is therefore now no condemnation to them which are in Christ Jesus, who walk not after the flesh, but after the Spirit. For the *law of the*

Spirit of life in Christ Jesus hath made me free from the law of sin and death."

It is indeed the *life* in the channel, not the channel, not even the *knowledge* of the life, but the actual *life* that encompasses salvation.

James speaks of this life as a perfect law in James 1:25, where He said, "But whoso looketh into the *perfect law of liberty*, and continueth therein, he being not a forgetful hearer, but a doer of the work, this man shall be blessed in his deed."

Jesus said plainly in John 15:5, "I am the vine, ye are the branches: He that abideth in Me, and I in him, the same bringeth forth much fruit: for *without Me ye can do nothing*." The life must be present.

It is sadly possible to remain only in the "knowledge of salvation" and not experience the Christ of salvation living in you. The difference, of course, is the absence or presence of, *life* ... Christ Himself.

29

Life in the Cross

To become a Christian, you must at least, understand the atonement of the Lord dying a substitutionary death on the cross for you, repent, and ask Him to come into your heart and save you. However, it is very possible to attend church, pray, read your Bible, and yet never understand what living the cross life is all about. Scripture declares the cross is the power of God.

There are many synonymous phrases in scripture depicting the cross life: being yoked with Christ, abiding in the vine, dying daily, entering the rest of God, eating His flesh and drinking His blood, walking in the Spirit, being one with Him, and He must increase and I must decrease. All of these imply one thing: union with Christ. You lose your life, so the life of Christ can be clearly expressed through you minus your flesh. You cease your own works, however good and well intentioned they are, so the Lord Himself may touch lives through you.

This whole concept is expressed beautifully in 2 Corinthians 4:10-12:

> "Always bearing about in the body the dying of the Lord Jesus, that the life also of Jesus might be made manifest in

our body. For we which live are always delivered unto death for Jesus' sake, that the life also of Jesus might be made manifest in our mortal flesh. So then death worketh in us, but life in you."

Death to self works *in us* that the life of Christ might work *through us*. It is the great exchange. What a swap!

This is the principle of the corn of wheat. Unless the seed falls into the ground and dies, it abides alone, but, if it dies, it brings forth much fruit (John 12:24). The seed will remain a seed if it stays in the seed bag, but the fruit will never be seen. The seed must trust the sower to disperse it, cover it, water it, and fertilize it until the elements work, causing the outer husk to slough off so that the life that has always been within can now be released to grow and produce a harvest.

Jesus died to bring many sons and daughters to this glory... to have the Son manifested in them. This cross life is a principle, the essential element, the fundamental truth concerning the power of God. You cannot grasp this or force it. It is lived out daily before the Lord.

Other religions promote a dying martyrdom. Christianity promotes a living martyrdom. Death works in us in order for life to work in others. When you understand this principle of the corn of wheat, death loses its sting, for you know He must increase and you must decrease. This is why Paul said, "I die daily." He knew the cross life to be an ongoing process as long as he lived in his earthly body.

Without living the cross life, we remain on the shoreline of Christianity, never experiencing the "breadth, length, depth, and height " of the love of Jesus Christ that surpasses knowledge about Him (Ephesians 3:18-19). We can be saved, but for the most part live powerless, without the cross life, for the cross *is the power of God* (1 Corinthians 1:18). It was for the joy set before Him that Jesus endured the cross (Hebrews 12:2). Once you see that dying to self is not for the sake of dying but for the sake of *living,* your heart will yearn to know Him more through His cross. To lose your life is indeed to gain *life*! This is what is meant to become a vessel of honor fit for the Master's use alone.

It is possible for us today as Christians to disregard the heir (Jesus) and desire only His inheritance, as in the parable of the vine dresser (Matthew 21:33-41). We can desire power, possessions, and position without submitting to the Son. There is an arrogance and pride in this that does not represent the nature of the Lord. Remember, that Jesus said His yoke would teach us that He was meek and lowly in heart. Daniel expressed it well in Daniel 11:14: "...the robbers of Thy people shall exalt themselves to establish the vision but they shall fail." There is no substitute for the nature of Christ or the will of God, regardless of supposed spiritual power.

30

Small Things

O nce I heard an old preacher say that big doors swing on little hinges. I have never forgotten the implications of that axiom.

Jesus spoke of the importance of the "small" in our lives when giving the parable of the unrighteous steward in Luke 16:1-13. His summation of the steward ended in verses 10-12, where He said:

> "He that is faithful in that which is least is faithful also in much: and he that is unjust in the least is unjust also in much. If therefore ye have not been faithful in the unrighteous mammon, who will commit to your trust the true riches? And if ye have not been faithful in that which is another man's, who shall give you that which is your own?"

The small reveals the absence, or presence of, the large.

A young preacher went to hear a "great man of God" speak. He took a seat by the aisle. It was a rainy day. The man sitting in front of the young preacher had placed his raincoat over the back of his seat. Part of the raincoat's hem lay in the aisle. As the speaker passed by, his muddy shoe stepped on the raincoat's edge. The "great man of

God" glanced down where he had stepped but kept on walking. The young preacher said that it mattered not what the message was, for the small had already revealed the absence of the large.

We are who we really are when there is no audience, no applause, no witness to what we do but God. Such is the place of "little things".

In Isaiah 45:3 the scripture reads ..."And I will give thee the treasures of darkness, and hidden riches of *secret places*, that thou mayest know that I, the Lord, which call thee by thy name, am the God of Israel."

The "secret places" reveal the hidden riches. There is honor that is to be sought from God only because He alone knows what has transpired beyond the sight of men (John 5:44).

Jesus spoke of the wise and faithful steward in Luke 12:22-48. He was speaking about the importance of watching for His return and living your life in a manner representing His Life in the Spirit.

In verses 43 and 44, Jesus said, "Blessed is that servant, whom his Lord when He cometh shall find so doing. Of a truth I say unto you, that He will make him ruler over all that he hath."

By position in the finished work of Christ, we have all, but by experience we still wait to see the "manifestation of the sons of God" (Romans 8:19). To those who are faithful in the small, the large will be under your rule when Christ returns. Big doors do indeed swing on little hinges!

31

Living after Death

When Christians lose a loved one who died in the faith, they can find great comfort in the scriptures concerning the present condition of that person's existence.

The account of the events that happened on the Mount of Transfiguration found in Luke 9:28-36 is very compelling and encouraging about life for the Christian once he departs this earth.

Jesus had taken Peter, James, and John up a mountain to pray. We know as Jesus prayed, His countenance was changed, and His clothing became white and glistering.

So often we just pass over verses 30 and 31, which read, "And, behold, there *talked with Him* two men, which were Moses and Elias: Who *appeared in glory*, and *spake of His decease* which He should accomplish in Jerusalem" (Luke 9:53-56).

Now, there are some wonderful things found in those two verses concerning a Christian's life after death. Moses and Elias (Greek for Elijah) had been dead for hundreds of years, yet here they are present "in glory" talking to Jesus! They were recognizable as themselves, or who they had been on earth. They were aware of current happenings on earth as they were speaking very specifically about what Jesus would soon accomplish in Jerusalem on the cross.

Jesus glistened, but they did not. All departed saints and those who are alive and remain at His coming, will be changed into their glorious, immortal bodies at His second coming (1 Corinthians 15:51-54).

Until our bodies are transformed from earthy to heavenly, we, as departed saints, join that glorious cloud of witnesses referred to in Hebrews 12:23 as "the spirits of just men made perfect." What a great group to be in!

Jesus Himself tells us about the departed saints being aware of events on earth in John 8:52-56. The disgruntled Jews were accusing Him of having devils. They brought up the subject in verses 52 and 53 that Abraham was dead. Jesus spoke to them about God the Father, then in verse 56 He made this amazing comment: "Your father Abraham rejoiced to see My day: and *he saw it, and was glad.*"

The Jews responded in verse 57, "Thou art yet fifty years old and hast Thou seen Abraham?"

To which Jesus replied wonderfully in verse 58, "Verily, verily, I say unto you, before Abraham was, I AM." He always existed, yet Abraham, now living "in the glory", was privy to the Lord's arrival as son of Mary in the form of a man. He rejoiced to see the earthly ministry of Jesus and knew what was about to transpire in Jerusalem. Yes, though Abraham had been dead for hundreds of years, *he rejoiced to see the Lord's day!*

All of those who compile that glorious group of witnesses, the spirits of just men made perfect, from Abraham all the way to your departed Christian loved ones, are all abuzz with excitement and anticipation of the next glorious event on the Lord's calendar... His second coming. What a day that will be!

Jesus also declares in Mark 12:26-27:

> "And as touching the dead, that they rise: have ye not read in the book of Moses, how in the bush God spake unto him, saying, 'I am the God of Abraham, and the God of Isaac, and the God of Jacob?' *He is not the God of the dead, but the God of the living*: ye therefore do greatly err."

Paul in 2 Corinthians 5:8 tells us, "We are confident, I say, and willing rather to be absent from the body, and to be *present with the Lord*."

These scriptures all comfort us who are believers in Christ. When we finish bearing the earthly here, we shall be present in "the glory" with the Lord. We shall be recognizable, capable of communication, emotions, cognizant of happenings on earth, and rejoicing as we wait for that glorious day of His return, for then we shall be like Him, changed in a moment, in the twinkling of an eye. We will also have a glorified body forever! (As I write this, I am approaching seventy, and the prospect of that glorified body is sounding more and more wonderful to me.)

32

Memorials

There are only two places in the New Testament where memorials are mentioned. Interestingly enough, these memorials are not made to God for something He has done, but rather, they are made by God in remembrance of something a woman and a man did. Quite amazing when you think about it, that two people could do something that so touched the heart of God that it was memorialized for ever in His mind and in scripture.

The first is recorded in Matthew 26:6-18. Jesus was in Bethany at the house of Simon the Leper. He was eating. A woman came with an alabaster box containing an expensive and precious ointment. She poured it on His head.

The disciples saw this act as a waste of money that could have been used to help the poor. Jesus rebuked the disciples for troubling the woman about what she had done for Him. He went on to say that she had done it for His burial. Then, in verse 13, He told them, "Verily I say unto you, wheresoever this gospel shall be preached in the whole world, there shall also this, that this woman hath done, be told for a *memorial of her*." Pretty special.

Jesus had repeatedly told His disciples what was about to happen to Him in Jerusalem, but they did not seem to understand; apparently, this woman did. She anointed Him with the best she had for His burial, and Jesus would always remember her act of sacrifice. It is interesting also to note that immediately after this, Judas "went unto the chief priests" (v.14) and from that time on, sought opportunity to betray Jesus.

The second act memorialized by God is found in Acts 10:1-48. Cornelius was a Roman soldier, a leader, stationed in Caesarea a few years after the death and resurrection of Jesus. Scripture says he was a devout man who feared God with all his house, gave much alms to the people, and prayed to God always. (v. 2). God sent an angel to Cornelius who told him in verse 4, "Thy prayers and thine alms are come up for a memorial before God." The angel gave Cornelius specific instructions to send men to Joppa and find Peter, who would tell Cornelius what to do.

Meanwhile, God was preparing Peter to receive Cornelius, who was not a Jew. Peter's heart was made ready to present the gospel to a Gentile. It is crucial to note that even though the prayers and alms of Cornelius were memorialized by God, he still needed the saving grace of the blood of Jesus. No good deeds will ever replace the need for personal salvation. Cornelius and his entire family received Christ as their Saviour.

Yet, in these two events, a woman and a Gentile, so touched the Lord and His Father that they are memorialized in scripture in a way that no one else was done, not even the apostles or prophets. What beautiful demonstrations of how God looks on the heart of each individual and his/her motivation for true worship. No prayers for greatness or power or position ... nothing but love. My, we have a lot to learn.

33

Offended at Him

It always amazes me that Jesus did no mighty work in His own country and among His own people (Mark 6:1-6). He healed a few sick folks and that was it. So much was His own amazement over this that in verse 6, scripture says, "And He marveled because of their unbelief. And He went round about their villages teaching."

Oh, they recognized that He spoke with wisdom and authority (v. 2). They even acknowledged some mighty works done by His hands, but then they recalled what they knew of the natural man Jesus. In verse 3, they said that this is that carpenter, Mary's son. His brothers are James, Joses, Judah, and Simon. His sisters live here. And they were *offended at Him*!

Jesus then made a sad comment in verse 4: "A prophet is not without honour, but in his own country, and among his own kin, and in his own house." His own family had thought Him "beside himself" on occasion. Perhaps this is where the old quote "Familiarity breeds contempt" ensues.

One great lesson to take out of all this exchange is this: never rule God out of the ordinary. They only saw Jesus as a regular guy. Yes,

He was a regular guy! He lived in a regular home with siblings and parents. He worked. He got weary. He got sleepy. He got hungry. He experienced every ordinary facet of ordinary living, so when you get tired and want to quit, He says, "I've been there." When you struggle through, barely getting by, He says, "I understand." When you are not appreciated for who you really are, He says, "I know." These are a few of the reasons He is our faithful High Priest, ever-living to make intercession for us. He gets it. He understands.

He simply did not come on the scene the way people thought He should. They failed to recognize Him as Son of God. They only saw him as Son of man. The marvel is, He is both Son of Man and Son of God. To recognize Him as only one to the exclusion of the other, places limitations where they are not meant to be. The limit is not on God's power to supply, but rather on our ability to receive.

Unbelief in Jesus as Son of Man limits our receiving His tender compassion as our Intercessor. Unbelief in Jesus as Son of God limits our receiving His power to change us, or our circumstances, or us through our circumstances. He came to be both ... compassionate Saviour, Friend, and sovereign, powerful God.

34

Our Gospel

M ore often than not, when we read the scriptures, the apostles and disciples referred to truth about the Lord as "the gospel of Jesus Christ". However, in 1 Thessalonians 1:5, Paul said, "For *our gospel* came not unto you in word only, but also in power, and in the Holy Ghost, and in much assurance; as ye know what manner of men we were among you for your sake."

"The gospel" was now "our gospel." There was now ownership and union with the Messenger and His message. "Our" meant acceptance of the terms, conditions, plans, expectations, results, demands, scope, and promises. Not only was the gospel that of Jesus, but now it was theirs ... total identification with the Owner of the gospel.

What follows the total identification with the Lord and His gospel is expressed in the rest of verse 5: not just words, but power, presence of the Holy Ghost, much assurance, and knowledge of who they were in Christ.

If we want to understand more of how we Christians can move from "the gospel" to "our gospel", we can prayerfully read all of

2 Corinthians 4, especially verses 11 and 12, which read, "For we which live are always delivered unto death for Jesus' sake, that the life also of Jesus might be made manifest in our mortal flesh. So then death worketh in us, but life in you."

Jesus speaks of this process also in John 12:23-26, where He said:

> "The hour is come, that the Son of man should be glorified. Verily, verily, I say unto you, except a corn of wheat fall into the ground and die, it abideth alone: but if it die, it bringeth forth much fruit. He that loveth his life shall lose it; and he that hateth his life in this world shall keep it unto life eternal. If any man serve Me, let him follow Me; and where I am, there shall also my servant be: if any man serve Me, him will My Father honour."

Here in this parable Jesus laid out the plan for "the gospel" becoming "our gospel". This is what Paul meant when he spoke in 2 Corinthians 4:10-12 about "death works in us, but life in you". If we want to see the power of God, the workings of the Holy Ghost, we cannot escape the way of the cross life. We may come with words, glorious words, scriptural words, but bondage, sickness, death, and demons retreat only before the presence of the Living Lord, not sympathy or good intentions.

Jesus said, "... for without Me, you can do nothing" (John 15:5). It is when we lose our life that we find Life. His manifest presence moves through us, and we see a difference made in the lives of others. Without Him, we can do nothing but talk about Him.

There are few today who want to really lay down their lives day in and day out. What we want is to have the Lord's blessing on how we want to live *our* lives, or we want to experience the power of God in order to be seen and esteemed by men. We want blessing and power without the Lord's dealing with the world, the flesh, and the devil that still operate in our lives even after salvation.

Once we understand the necessity of not just being saved by the cross, but actually living *in* the cross, we will never be the same again. Our little corn of wheat falls in the ground as well. With just the right amount of heat, light, and water, we find something wonderful taking place; His life springs up in place of ours in the most remarkable ways. His gospel becomes our gospel, and there is no confusion about who is the Great One.

35

Our Own "I AM" Moment

In Exodus 3:14, Moses queried God concerning His name and how he should respond when asked by His people about Him. God's reply about His name in verse 14 was, "And God said unto Moses, 'I AM THAT I AM', and He said, 'Thus shalt thou say unto the children of Israel, 'I AM hath sent me unto you.' "

Of course, we know that declaration of God's name signified He is *eternal* with no beginning and no end. He is the Perfect Holy One who has always been, and always shall be, God with all power and authority in heaven and earth.

Jesus had His compelling "I AM" moment in John 8:56-58. The Jews were accusing Him of having a devil. Jesus brought up the subject of their father Abraham, telling them in verse 56 that Abraham rejoiced to see the day of Jesus and was glad.

The Jews were livid. They argued that Jesus was not even fifty years old and how then could He have seen Abraham? In verse 58, Jesus said, "Verily, verily, I say unto you, Before Abraham was, I AM." Wow!

In that one statement, Jesus declared His equality in the Godhead. He too ever existed, and has no beginning or end. Jesus *is* God.

Nowhere is this more clearly written by inspiration of God than in Colossians 1:14-19, where scripture declares all things were created by Him and for Him. Jesus is before all things and by Him all things consist. Jesus is very God of very God! To deny the "I AM" of Jesus Christ is to miss the mark completely.

Of all the New Testament writers, surely none could be more credited with explaining the gospel than Paul. He called himself a "pattern" of the grace of God, having received such mercy from God since he so persecuted the church, even holding the coats of those who stoned Stephen to death.

Paul's amazing conversion experience in Acts 9, his "chosen vessel" calling, the special miracles performed through him, the numerous sufferings, shipwrecks, beatings, imprisonments, and eventual death as a martyr certainly qualify Paul to give us a great example of what should be our "I AM" moment as believers.

Paul wrote to Timothy in 1 Timothy 1:15, saying, "This is a faithful saying, and worthy of all acceptation, that Christ Jesus came into the world to save sinners; of whom I AM chief." Paul never lost sight of where he had been before Christ. He did not say "I was chief" of sinners, but rather "I AM chief". On this side of heaven, there is great safety in remembering I AM chief of sinners.

In Romans 7:23-25, Paul addressed another law that wars against the Spirit in us. He said, "But I see another law in my members, warring against the law of my mind, and bringing me into captivity to the law of sin which is in my members. O wretched man that I AM! who shall deliver me from the body of this death? I thank God through Jesus Christ our Lord. So then with the mind I myself serve the law of God; but with the flesh the law of sin."

Paul did not say, "I was wretched" but rather, "I *am* wretched". On this side of the second coming of Jesus, there is great safety in knowing that I *am* wretched and can serve the law of flesh and death, though still a believer.

In Galatians 2:19-20, Paul gives us the crowning glory of our "I *am*" *reality:*

> "For I through the law am dead to the law, that I might live unto God. *I am crucified with Christ*: nevertheless I live, yet not I, but Christ liveth in me: and the life which I now live in the flesh I live by the faith of the Son of God, who loved me, and gave himself for me."

Throughout all ages, there is great safety in knowing that *I am* crucified with Christ!

Knowing I *am* chief of sinners, knowing I *am* wretched, and knowing I *am* crucified with Christ, keeps us in the humble place of 1 Corinthians 1:26-31 which describes our calling perfectly:

> "For ye see your calling, brethren, how that not many wise men after the flesh, not many mighty, not many noble, are called: But God hath chosen the foolish things of the world to confound the wise; and God hath chosen the weak things of the world to confound the things which are mighty; And base things of the world, and things which are despised, hath God chosen, yea, and things which are not, to bring to nought things that are: That *no flesh* should glory in His presence. But of Him are ye in Christ Jesus, who of God is made unto us wisdom, and righteousness,

and sanctification, and redemption: That according as it is written, He that glorieth, let him glory in the Lord."

If you have your "I AM'S" sorted out, you will never have to be concerned about misplaced credit or glory. God can safely use you then without ruining you or spoiling His plans.

36

Patmos

The apostle John tells us in Revelation 1:9 why he had been banished to the Isle of Patmos. "I, John, who also am your brother, and companion in tribulation, and in the kingdom and patience of Jesus Christ, was in the isle that is called Patmos, for the word of God, and for the testimony of Jesus Christ."

Patmos is a small, rocky, treeless Greek island in the Aegean Sea. It is a little over thirteen square miles in size. Today Patmos has a population of around three thousand. In John's day, probably few or none were there.

According to ancient history, the Romans often sent prisoners to islands. Whether John was actually sent to Patmos in exile or banishment really does not matter as we know he told us why he was there ... "for the word of God and the testimony of Jesus Christ".

Now, this statement of John has a dual meaning. He was certainly there because he preached the word of God and held the testimony of Jesus Christ, but he was also there to receive the word of God and *give* the testimony of Jesus Christ ... the great Revelation of Jesus Christ and the events that would take place on the earth and in the heavens.

Revelation 1:1-2 tells us God gave this revelation to Jesus, who gave it to His angel, who gave it to John, who gave it to us ... a glorious hand-me-down!

In looking up the meaning of the word "Patmos", several definitions come up, all with the same general meaning of difficulty: to tread or walk on, squeezed to pieces, my killing, my mortality. John wasn't on Patmos for a vacation. It was a difficult island on which to survive.

What is interesting to note is the total lack of information John gives us about Patmos and what it was like trying to exist while there. No details are given about having to find some place to shelter or how he found food. No word at all about his physical suffering while there other than his saying he was a "companion in tribulation" (Revelation 1:9).

John did not enshrine the way he got to where he was ... "in the Spirit on the Lord's day" hearing (Revelation1:10). Now, we would have written a book about how terribly we suffered on our Patmos. We would have stood and given lengthy testimony about our trials and tribulations. John remained silent on his sufferings and wrote on the revelation. Amen!

It is a good thing to share how the Lord has brought you through your own Patmos experience. It is another thing to enshrine your suffering and visit it like a place of worship. We suffer not for the sake of suffering. Our Patmos, our place of squeezing, of being tread upon, of dying to self is for the same thing as that of John ... for the word of God and the testimony of Jesus Christ. Indeed!

John reckoned, as we should, "that the sufferings of this present time are not worthy to be compared with the glory which shall be revealed in us" (Romans 8:18).

37

Pressing and Walking

In Philippians 3:13-16, Paul writes:

> "Brethren, I count not myself to have apprehended: but this one thing I do, forgetting those things which are behind, and reaching forth unto those things which are before, I *press* toward the mark for the prize of the high calling of God in Christ Jesus. Let us therefore, as many as be perfect, be thus minded: and if in any thing ye be otherwise minded, God shall reveal even this unto you. Nevertheless, whereto we have already attained, let us *walk* by the same rule, let us mind the same thing."

The normal Christian life is to be one of *walking in what we know and pressing toward more of His life. We walk. We press.*

There should be no stopping point in this journey of faith. There should be no place where you plant your feet and feel you have arrived. As long as we are in these bodies, the movement should always be "to grow up into Him in all things, which is the Head, even Christ" (Ephesians 4:15).

Our walk should always be one of following on to know the Lord (Hosea 6:3). It is always a going forward on our journey after a godly sort (3 John 1:6). We should constantly "grow in grace and in the knowledge of the Lord" (2 Peter 3:18). We are actually "instructed both to be full and to be hungry " (Philippians 4:12).

What keeps us from pressing on in Christ? Have we become like Moab in Jeremiah 48:11? "Moab hath been at ease from his youth, and he hath settled on his lees, and hath not been emptied from vessel to vessel, neither hath he gone into captivity: therefore his taste remained in him, and his scent is not changed." We need to be poured from "vessel to vessel", or as it is expressed in the New Testament, changed from "glory to glory" (2 Corinthians 3:18).

What holds us back? Have we built "tabernacles" as Peter suggested doing on the Mount of Transfiguration, and refuse to hear what the beloved Son is saying (Matthew 17:4-5)? Perhaps our "tabernacles", whatever they may be, make us feel safe and comfortable, and like the people of Israel, we just want our "Moses" to go to the mount and hear what God has to say instead of us. If we hear for ourselves, then we will have to do something. It is so much easier just not to hear, to stay on our lees, to not be changed from glory to glory. How very sad is that.

Once a dear brother was preaching. He held up an apple seed and reminded us that within that small seed lay the potential for another tree and much fruit. The tree and fruit were there waiting. The seed was waiting for the forces of nature to bring it forward. The seed would fall in the ground and die in order for this to happen.

Christ, the Hope of Glory, is within us. What precious seed is that! We should walk in that great truth, but continue to press toward the blessed hope of "growing up into Him in all things". We walk. We press. We should always be going forward in Him.

The scripture encourages us that change should be happening. John 3:30 gives us this succinctly, "He must increase, but I *must* decrease." If the Lord is not increasing in us, the fault lies with us, certainly not Him.

Psalm 37:4-5 tells us, "Delight thyself also in the Lord; and He *shall* give thee the desires of thine heart. Commit thy way unto the Lord; trust also in Him; and He shall bring it to pass." He loves for us to long for Him, to desire for Him to live through us. This is one prayer that is *always* answered in the affirmative. We walk in what we know of Him. We press toward more.

38

Seeing Jesus for Yourself

Seeing Jesus for yourself, not just hearing about Him, but actually "seeing", understanding who He is, is a transforming experience. You can never be the same once you begin to see Him.

Seeing Him starts at your initial conversion in faith, but it should happen over and over again as you "follow on to know the Lord" (Hosea 6:3) and are changed from "glory to glory" as we behold His glory (2 Corinthians 3:18).

The Samaritan woman at the well in John 4 "saw" Jesus and ran to tell others. Indeed, Christ openly spoke of His divinity to her for when she spoke to Him about the coming Messiah, He replied by saying, "I that speak unto thee am He" (John 4:26).

Instead of her well water, the woman took this revelation about Jesus back to the city and told others about Him. Truly seeing Jesus for who He is always has this effect. "For we cannot but speak the things which *we have seen and heard*" (Acts 4:20).

John 4:39 tells us that many of the Samaritans believed on Jesus just because of what this woman said about Him. Her testimony must have been very compelling, as she stressed that Jesus knew everything she had done in her life.

The Samaritans went to Jesus, asking Him to tarry there, which He did for two days, speaking to them about the things of God. John 4:41-42 states, "And many more believed because of His own word; And said unto the woman, 'Now we believe, not because of thy saying: for *we have heard Him for ourselves, and know* that this is indeed the Christ, the Saviour of the world.'" These people had made the transition from hearing about Jesus to "seeing" Him for themselves.

No scripture expresses more exactly what transpires in our hearts if we do indeed "see Christ" than that found in Job 42:5-6. Job says, "I have heard of Thee by the hearing of the ear: but now mine eye seeth Thee. Wherefore I abhor myself, and repent in dust and ashes."

Job gives us the "seeing" who God is with the corresponding response of recognizing what we are apart from Him. Thus we realize the need of repentance and acceptance of His life in exchange for ours. This of course is the very essence of the gospel of Jesus Christ.

Whenever we see the "brightness of His glory and the express image of His person", our reaction will always be the revelation that we are not just in darkness, but we are in fact darkness apart from Him (Ephesians 5:8). The man or woman who understands this won't have to pretend humility. True humility is a direct result of "seeing Jesus as He is" and our own corresponding lack.

Paul says in Philippians 2:9-10, "Wherefore God also hath highly exalted Him, and given Him a name which is above every name: That at the name of Jesus every knee should bow, of things in heaven, and things in earth, and things under the earth."

Now, we have glimpses of Him because we "see through a glass darkly but then face to face. Now I know in part but then shall I know even as also I am known" (1 Corinthians 13:12).

However, even though we do not see Him in fullness yet, the glimpses that we do have as we "see Him" will continue to humble us and change us from one glory to another.

The greatest and final glory is wonderfully explained in 1 John 3:2-3, where John says, "Beloved, now are we the sons of God, and it *doth not yet appear what we shall be* : but we know that, when He shall appear, we *shall be like Him; for we shall see Him as He is,* And every man that hath this hope in him purifieth himself, even as He is pure." Amen!

39

Slain Before

Revelation 13:8 gives us an amazing statement about the Lord Jesus. It is given within the context of scriptures explaining the Antichrist and his moment on the earth.

Verse 8 reads, "And all that dwell upon the earth shall worship him, (Antichrist), whose names are not written in the book of life of the Lamb (Jesus) *slain from the foundation of the world.*"

Jesus, slain before the world was even created? How can this be? I have read some scholars believe this statement is a misprint in the King James Version of the Bible. I certainly don't believe that since the answer to the puzzle is given clearly in 1 Peter 1:18-20. Peter is instructing the scattered church about their redemption in Christ. He says:

> "Forasmuch as ye know that ye were not redeemed with corruptible things, as silver and gold, from your vain conversation received by tradition from your fathers; But with the precious blood of Christ, as of a lamb without blemish and without spot: Who verily was *foreordained before the foundation of the world*, but was *manifest* in these *last times for you.*"

God the Father, being the Eternal "I AM" (Exodus 3:14), and Jesus Christ, being the Eternal "I AM" (John 8:58), know the end from the beginning. They are Alpha and Omega. They exist in the great eternal *now*. There is no time with them. They are not waiting for things to happen. They speak of things that are not to us because they are to them. We see evidence of this in Revelation 10:6, which speaks to us that "time should be no more".

We are the ones who currently live in time and space. Because of this, there must be what scripture refers to as "fullness of time", "set time", or "due season". The Triune God knew from the beginning of His creation that the man He made in His image would go astray. God interjected Himself into our time and space as the remedy, providing Himself as the Lamb without spot, wrinkle, or blemish.

Jesus is now eternally seated at the right hand of the Majesty on high, ever living to make intercession for us. He knows full well that He is going to enter our time and space yet again when He comes to gather His Church. Then we also will have bodies like unto His glorious body, and time and space will forever change for us. We will no longer be waiting for things to happen. We too will be existing in the eternal I AM of God!

Until then, we have the wonderful ministry of the Great Comforter, the Holy Spirit, that Jesus sent to us after His ascension. The Holy Spirit teaches, comforts, guides, and corrects us as we continue in time and space, waiting patiently and expectantly for the second coming of our Lord.

We are comforted by the knowledge that Jesus, in His pre-existent Life with God, knew the end from the beginning, knew the position of being slain, which He would indeed live out within the confines of our time and space, all for the will of God and love for us. Praise the Lamb of glory!

40

Such a Man

In Matthew 26:17-19, Jesus and His disciples were preparing to eat the Passover meal together. When the disciples asked Jesus where they would eat the Passover, Jesus responded in verse 18 by saying, "Go into the city to *such a man,* and say unto him, 'The Master saith, My time is at hand. I will keep the Passover at thy house with My disciples.'" The disciples did as Jesus had told them, and the plans were made.

The man who owned the home where Jesus and His disciples celebrated the Passover was simply referred to in scripture as "such a man". His name is not even given, but Jesus knew him. He knew his heart. He knew the answer to His request would be in the affirmative.

It was enough for this "such a man" that the Master had said, "My time is at hand". Jesus needed to use his home on short notice, and He got it. No great accolades or even name recognition here, just willingness for divine opportunity to present itself. How wonderful it must be to the Lord's heart to know "such a man" today who quietly goes about living close to Him, ready to be called upon at a moment's notice for inconspicuous service.

In Luke 19:29-35, we find a similar event in scripture. Jesus has a specific need once again. He needs a donkey upon which to ride into Jerusalem. He tells His disciples in verses 30-31:

> "Go ye into the village over against you; in the which at your entering ye shall find a colt tied, whereon yet never man sat: loose him, and bring him hither. And if *any man* ask you, 'Why do ye loose him?' thus shall ye say unto him, 'Because the Lord hath need of him.'"

The disciples once again did as Jesus instructed. They found the colt tied and began to loose him. The "owners" asked what they were doing. Their reply was simple in verse 34, "And they said, 'The Lord has need of him.'" That was all it took! Jesus knew some donkey owners as well!

These men who owned the colt do not have their names recorded in scripture either. They sought no great appreciation or recognition. They just gave their colt to the disciples because the Lord had need of him.

In John 5:41-44, Jesus said:

> "I receive not honour from men. But I *know you*, that ye have not the love of God in you. I am come in my Father's name, and ye receive Me not: if another shall come in his own name, him ye will receive. How can ye believe, which receive honour one of another, and *seek not the honour that cometh from God only*?"

Jesus knew the man in whose home He wanted to celebrate the Passover. He knew the ones who owned the donkey that He needed to ride into Jerusalem. He knew them, and He knew giving them name recognition was not a requirement for their obedience. How wonderful!

41

The Captain

J esus was one with the Father, not just during His earthly life but
throughout all eternity past, present, future. The only time their
union was broken, was the hours on the cross when Jesus became
our sin offering. That was also the only time Jesus used the name
God instead of Father. Jesus is the Word of God. He gives expression
of the Godhead so that we might understand. He already knows,
of course. He is the express image of God's person. This is all for
our benefit.

Over and over during His earthly ministry, Jesus said He did only the
things His Father showed Him. He would say, "The Father worketh
hitherto, and I work" (John 5:17). They were one in purpose and
in plan. He was, and is, the Lamb slain from the foundation of the
world (Revelation 13:8). His purpose in coming was set in God's
heart and His from the beginning of creation.

Jesus set His face steadfastly, scripture says, to go to Jerusalem and
fulfill God's will. He was determined, having explained to His
disciples on several occasions just what would happen there. They
followed on with Him in fear and amazement, not understanding at
all what was about to happen in the spiritual realm. Even the angels

would be amazed and wonder. However, the Father and the Son had known the plan since the foundation of the world, and now, the fullness of time was here. The plan was put into operation.

Scripture says in John 18:4, "Jesus therefore, *knowing all things* that should come upon Him, went forth and said unto them, 'Whom seek ye?'" Why then the awful struggle in Gethsemane? Why then the statement that He learned obedience by the things He suffered? What did He who was slain before the foundation of the world have to learn about obedience?

Jesus learned. He experienced the cost of obedience in the human experience. He tasted the gripping agony of human struggle before sovereign God. He did this as High Priest, once again, who is touched by reason of our infirmities. He knows by vicarious experience what obedience feels like for a human being in the face of supreme sorrow and emotional pain. He learned it in a human body as Son of Man. He experienced it on our behalf, and because of this, He will help us through the most gut-wrenching choices, or experiences, we will have in our human lives. "For it became Him, for whom are all things, and by whom are all things, in bringing many sons unto glory, to make the Captain of their salvation perfect through sufferings" (Hebrews 2:10). Oh, the Captain of our salvation! Thank You.

42

Authority in Submission

Many times the scripture found in James 4:7 is only half quoted as, "Resist the devil and he will flee from you." However, the first part sets the premise by which the second is concluded: "Submit yourselves therefore to God. Resist the devil and he will flee from you." Submission to God comes before successful resistance. Submission to God in humility is where the power lies.

The devil knows and recognizes God's authority, not our imitation of it. I remember one dear saint saying that he'd rather have the recognition of demons than the praise of men. That statement may first sound suspicious until you read Acts 19:14-17 and Luke 4:34 and 41.

Sceva was a Jew and chief of the priests. He had seven sons who were very impressed that Jesus could cast out evil spirits with just a word. They decided to try the same thing invoking Jesus's name. The man in whom the evil spirit was, successfully overpowered all seven of Sceva's sons and sent them away running for their lives, naked and wounded. The key is in verse 15: "And the evil spirit answered and said, 'Jesus I know and Paul I know but who are you?'"

The evil spirits recognized the authority of God, not only in Jesus, but also in Paul. They did not have to be told; they knew. They still do. Authority in the spirit is not something to be snatched like a gift under a Christmas tree. Authority, true authority from God, comes by being yoked together with Christ, for it is Christ that the enemy recognizes as the victor.

The Lord makes a very sobering statement in Matthew 7:22-23: "Many will say to me in that day, 'Lord, Lord, have we not prophesied in Thy name? and in Thy name cast out devils? and in Thy name done many wonderful works?' And then will I profess unto them, 'I never *knew* you: depart from Me, ye that work iniquity,' " I never knew you...wow!

Successful service is never proof of ministry. True service comes only from knowing the Lord and moving as He directs. How is that accomplished? The answer is found in Matthew 11:28-30:

> "Come unto Me, all ye that labour and are heavy laden, and I will give you rest. Take my yoke upon you, and learn of Me; for I am meek and lowly in heart: and ye shall find rest unto your souls. For My yoke is easy, and My burden is light."

A yoke restricts. It binds you one to the other so you cannot move independently. Where one goes, the other goes. Where one does not go, neither goes the other.

Jesus only worked when the Father worked. He was yoked. He did not move independently of the Father. He said He only did the things His Father told Him. Do we?

Over and over in John 17, the Lord prays that we may be one in Him and in the Father. One, so yoked, so much in unison that we move together. This union is recognized instantly by the devil and his demons. There is no substitution for it. "Nevertheless the foundation of God standeth sure, having this seal, The Lord knoweth them that are His. And Let every one that nameth the name of Christ depart from iniquity" (2 Timothy 2:19). Jesus knows who are yoked with Him, and so does the enemy.

Problems arise when we wriggle out of the yoke and move here and there independent of the Lord. Then when we meet with failure, we wonder what happened. This worked before, but now it doesn't! More than likely, we left the yoke, and thus we left the authority of God.

There is only one thing that will keep us yoked with Christ. Second Corinthians 5:14 says, "For the love of Christ *constraineth* us." Think of what "constrain" means: to severely restrict the scope, extent, or activity of; to limit, curb, or check. Only love can do that. His love, and our love for Him, is the one element, the glue, that keeps us yoked, and thus engaged in the authority of God, that is recognized by devils and feared by man.

43

The Deeds of the Nicolaitans

H ate is a strong word. Not only does it imply great dislike, but it means to detest, to have an extreme aversion to. Hate is a serious word not to be used lightly, or thrown around in conversation simply because we are annoyed.

Jesus used the word *"hate"* twice in the book of the Revelation (Revelation 2:6 and 15), both times referring to the same thing ... the deeds and doctrine of the Nicolaitans. Each time Jesus used the word *"hate"* while speaking to the church at Ephesus and the church in Pergamos. He was addressing believers, not the world. And, yes, He used the word *"hate"*, not toward the people but toward their deeds, and the doctrine of those who professed they were believers in these churches.

What were the deeds and doctrines of these Christians that Jesus so strongly opposed? Simply stated, the Nicolaitans believed it was acceptable for Christians to practice immorality and consume food offered to idols. If it feels good, do it. God loves you. Grace will cover it. Go ahead. Enjoy yourself. Sound familiar?

Second Peter 3:16 tells us that within some scriptures, "… are things hard to be understood, which they that are unlearned and unstable wrest, as they do also the other scriptures, unto their own destruction." Romans 6:15 states, "What then? Shall we sin, because we are not under the law, but under grace? God forbid."

It is a serious thing for Christians to willfully continue to practice immorality. Thank God, He gives us "space to repent" even as He gave Jezebel in Revelation 2:20-22. This Jezebel was doing the exact same thing as the Nicolaitans and teaching others to do the same … commit fornication and eat food sacrificed to idols.

Jesus hated the deeds, not the people committing the deeds. He also said He hated the doctrine the Nicolaitans held. The doctrine taught by so called Christians to others was in the name of religion … go ahead, do this. God is a God of love. It's okay. It is not okay. Jesus is the same yesterday, today, and forever. He has not changed since He inspired the writing of John the Revelator. He still hates the deeds and doctrines of the Nicolaitans no matter the age in which they live. We do well if we agree with Him.

44

The DNA of Jesus

The gospel is simple. In 2 Corinthians 11:3, Paul said, "But I fear, lest by any means, as the serpent beguiled Eve through his subtlety, so your minds should be corrupted from the simplicity that is in Christ." Man is the one who muddies the waters and complicates the matter of salvation. Briefly stated ... we died in Christ. Believe it. Repent. Receive Christ. You are born again, and the Spirit of Christ comes to live in you to work out what has been placed within ... His life.

Jesus had to come as Son of Man. He had to have a human body and human heredity. He had to have humankind's DNA, his genetic code, his connection to Adam's race. He took all of the first man (Adam) in Him to the cross reconciling the entire human race unto holy God. That is miracle number one. Then comes miracle number two.

Paul says it this way in Colossians 1:27: "...Christ *in you*, the hope of glory." Us in Christ then Christ in us ... the great exchange! And again in Romans 5:10, Paul said, "For if, when we were enemies, we were reconciled to God by the death of His Son, much more, *being reconciled, we shall be saved by His life.*"

How do we get from point A to point B? All the good works, all the best we can muster, cannot bridge this great divide. Scripture is emphatic on this point. You *must* be born again. You *must* receive the DNA, the genetic code, the actual life of Jesus. His Spirit *must* come to live in you. It is a real event. You were born of Adam's race and received the DNA of your parents. Now, you *must* be born of the Spirit and receive the DNA of Jesus.

The Father will only recognize the life of His Son in you as qualification to live in heaven.

> "The first man (Adam) is of the earth, earthy. The second man is the Lord from Heaven. As is the earthy, such are they also that are earthy: and as is the heavenly, such are they also that are heavenly. And as we have borne the image of the earthy, we shall *also bear the image of the heavenly.* Now this I say, brethren, that flesh and blood *cannot inherit* the kingdom of God; neither doth corruption inherit incorruption "(1 Corinthians 15:47-50).

Flesh and blood cannot live in the kingdom of heaven. It would be like trying to live on the moon minus the space suit. Impossible. The natural man failed to remain under the headship of eternal God. He failed. He sinned, and that propensity to continue in sin was forever naturally and genetically linked to us who are born on this earth. We gravitate to it. You don't have to teach a child to lie, be selfish, or fling a fit. It is a natural outcome of the nature within.

Only the grace of God and the raising by decent parents can keep people from becoming what Acts 17:5 refers to as "lewd fellows of the baser sort". Even if we are the "more noble" as referenced in Acts 17:11, it simply doesn't matter. Whether we are a "lewd fellow" or a "more noble fellow", the fact remains: the natural man cannot inherit the things of the Spirit of God. You must be born again. We must be born again to receive the forgiveness of God through the reconciling work of the cross of Christ, to be birthed through the Spirit and receive the life, the genetic code, the DNA of Jesus.

Science thinks it a great thing when man can use the DNA of a sheep to clone that sheep. (I have read, however, that cloned animals age quickly and die early. Oh, well.) That amazing process of cloning is one grain of sand on a beach compared to what will happen when ... "the Lord Himself shall descend from heaven with a shout, with the voice of the archangel, and with the trump of God: and the dead *in Christ* shall rise first: Then we which are alive and remain shall be caught up together with them in the clouds, to meet the Lord in the air: and so shall we ever be with the Lord" (1Thessalonians 4:16-17).

Jesus will call for those who share His Spirit, His DNA, His genetic code. Works cannot touch this. Good deeds won't matter. If He didn't know you in this life, if you never received Him as Lord and Saviour, if you don't have His DNA, you'll never leave the ground!

"In a moment, in the twinkling of an eye, at the last trump: for the trumpet shall sound, and the dead shall be raised incorruptible, and we shall be changed" (1 Corinthians 15:52).

At the present time, those who have been born again have what scripture calls "the earnest of our inheritance UNTIL the redemption of the purchased possession" (Ephesians 1:14). Those who have His Life, His DNA, His genetic code will get the finishing touch ... a body like unto His glorious body. Oh, praise the Lord! "Who shall change our vile body, that it may be fashioned like unto His glorious body, according to the working whereby *He is able even to subdue all things unto Himself*" (Philippians 3:21).

No wonder scripture tells us not to ... "neglect so great salvation" in Hebrews 2:3. One would think that all people would come in droves to Christ to receive such a great gift, this pearl of great price, but that is not the case. The natural man does not desire the things of God, for they are foolishness to him. You have to experience salvation to understand it. That leap from the natural to the spiritual is what faith is all about.

45

The First Song

One day I was thinking about the art of singing. I asked the Lord, "What was the first song ever sung?" Much to my amazement, a scripture came quickly to my mind, almost simultaneously, as though He was waiting for me to ask so He could give the answer.

The first song was sung during creation. In Job 38:6-7, God said in speaking to Job about the creation of the universe, "Whereupon are the foundations thereof fastened? or who laid the corner stone thereof; When *the morning stars sang together,* and all the sons of God (angels) shouted for joy?" (I assume this was also the first shout!)

In this scripture God is answering Job out of the whirlwind. Actually, His reply to Job's bewilderment, is a series of questions that center around the same theme that is expressed by God in verses 3-4, "Gird up now thy loins like a man; for I will demand of thee, and answer thou Me. Where wast thou when I laid the foundations of the earth? Declare, if thou hast understanding."

It is a complete mystery to me how any thinking human being can look around at this planet and even for one moment question creation. There is such a myriad of life all interconnected and responding together in a great chorus of seasonal patterns that we cannot initiate or cease. There is simply too much intricate design, from the world we see to the microscopic we can't see, to have crawled up from the ooze, or burst forth from some big bang. In Psalm 14:1, David said it plainly, " The fool hath said in his heart, 'There is no God.'"

The account of creation found in Genesis 1:1-31, is interspersed seven times with God's pronouncements. In the first six pronouncements, God said of His creation, "It was good." In the last pronouncement in verse 31, God says, "It was very good." The morning stars sang together, and all the sons of God shouted for joy!

Now, here is the wonder and the marvel to me ... the angels understood the creation of the universe and the earth in particular, but they cannot sing and shout over God's sacrifice of Jesus for our sin. In 1 Peter 1:12, we are told concerning the gospel... "which things the angels desire to look into."

Also, in 1 Corinthians 4:9, Paul stated, "... for we are made a spectacle unto the world, and *to angels*, and to men." Not being human, not having the inherited nature of Adam, angels simply cannot grasp our joy in being born again by the Spirit of God.

We are the ones who should sing and shout for the great redemption that has been created in us through the precious blood of Jesus Christ! No one can sing this song but the redeemed. And when we do, our voices join in chorus with all saints throughout the ages echoing God's pronouncements: "It is good. It is *very good*!" That is something worth singing and shouting about!

46

The True Witness

In Acts 22:6-18, Paul is recounting to his Jewish captors his defense; his conversion experience to faith in Christ. In verses 14 and 15, Paul relates to them what Ananias, a devout man according to the law, told him about God's choosing him for service.

In verse 14 Paul gives them Ananias's statement, "And he said, 'The God of our fathers hath chosen thee, that thou shouldest *know* His will and *see* that Just One and shouldest *hear* the voice of His mouth. For thou shalt be *His witness* unto all men of *what thou hast seen and heard.*'"

A true witness can only testify to that of which he, or she, has actually seen, heard, or been a part of. Anything else is secondhand information and lacks the zeal of shared participation.

In Psalm 45:1-2, scripture says, "My heart is indicting a good matter: I speak of the *things which I have made touching the king ....*" It simply is impossible to "touch" King Jesus and not have your own personal testimony enabling you to become a *true witness* to the things you have seen and heard.

When we touch His life in our circumstances, when we are in union with Him, when we abide in the vine, then we have testimony, a true witness to the things that have been made *in* us through vital contact *with Him*.

This is what is meant in Acts 4:13, when scripture says, "Now when they saw the boldness of Peter and John, and perceived that they were unlearned and ignorant men, they marveled; and they took knowledge of them, that they had been with Jesus." This kind of witness touches lives inwardly, not just the mind but the spirit. This witness is being salt and makes others thirsty to drink and taste of the Lord for themselves. This witness reveals light and shines on the way, illuminating the path for others who may be stumbling in darkness.

The true witness is expressed again in Acts 3:6, where Peter tells the lame man who is asking for alms at the temple gate, "Then Peter said, 'Silver and gold have I none; but *such as I have give I thee*: In the name of Jesus Christ of Nazareth rise up and walk.'" Such as I have ... such as we have ... that is what we can give.

The greatest statement on being a true witness is, of course, from the Lord Himself. In Acts 26:14-18, Paul is recalling his conversion experience to King Agrippa. He quotes the Lord's words to him:

> "And when we were all fallen to the earth, I heard a voice speaking unto me, and saying in the Hebrew tongue, 'Saul, Saul, why persecutest thou Me? It is hard for thee to kick against the pricks.' And I said, 'Who art thou, Lord?' And He said, 'I am Jesus whom thou persecutest. But rise, and stand upon thy feet: for I have appeared unto thee for this purpose, to make thee a minister and a *witness both of these things which thou hast seen, and of those things in the which I will appear unto thee*; Delivering thee from the people, and

from the Gentiles, unto whom now I send thee, To open their eyes, and to turn them from darkness to light, and from the power of Satan unto God, that they may receive forgiveness of sins, and inheritance among them which are sanctified by faith that is in Me.'"

This kind of "true witness" will usually bring about certain responses from the listeners: they will either with great heart longing draw close to the Lord for themselves, or they will turn on you in anger, despising the truth.

Once you touch the risen Lord, like Peter and John in Acts 4:20, you "cannot but speak *the things which we have seen and heard.*" John also said in 1 John 1:1, "That which was from the beginning, which we have heard, which we have seen with our eyes, which we have looked upon, and *our hands have handled of the Word of life ... .*" What you have actually experienced of the Lord's life becomes your testimony, not just words about Him. Hearts will be changed. Lives will be touched because you have become a witness to His very Life and are now enabled to give testimony to the Truth.

47

The Worship of Two Women

In Matthew 26:6-13, and Mark 14:3-8, scripture gives us the beautiful example of worship given by a woman. In both Matthew and Mark, this woman remains nameless. She pours precious ointment on the head of Jesus with no mention of His feet.

In Luke 7:37-48, scripture tells us of a sinful woman who came crying and anointing the feet of Jesus, as well as His head, expressing great repentance and love for Him. John 11:1-2 indicates this woman who did these things was Mary, the sister of Martha and Lazarus of Bethany. More than likely all of these events are one and the same, and the woman is Mary of Bethany.

The worship of this woman so touched the heart of Jesus that He pronounced in Matthew 26:13, "Verily I say unto you, Wheresoever this gospel shall be preached in the whole world, there shall also this, that this woman hath done, be told for a *memorial of her.*" I am sure this shocked the disciples, who were more concerned at this point about who would be the greatest among them! After all, there was no mention of a memorial to be told for them.

This Mary came to Jesus not asking for anything. She came humbly before Him with no pretense or request. She came with understanding of His mission that the disciples did not appear to have even though Jesus had told them repeatedly what was going to happen to Him in Jerusalem. Jesus affirmed Mary's understanding when He said in Matthew 26:12, "For in that she hath poured this ointment on My body, she did it for My burial."

True worship comes with understanding of the One being worshiped. Only when you begin to "see Him as He is" will you fall on your knees before Him in realization of your own sinfulness and His complete holiness, as Peter did in Luke 5:8. The thought of asking for something never enters the mind in this kind of worship, for adoration of Him overwhelms personal need.

Such was the worship of this Mary of Bethany. Her worship so touched the heart of Jesus that He memorialized the event because of it. He did this to such a degree that He even said, *"Wheresoever this gospel shall be preached in the whole world, there shall also this, that this woman hath done, be told for a memorial of her"* (Matthew 26:13). Now that is truly remarkable!

Another woman whose worship is also mentioned in scripture is the mother of James and John, the wife of Zebedee. Her name was Salome. In Matthew 20:17-24 scripture tells us Jesus had explained to His disciples the events which were about to happen to Him: betrayal, condemnation, crucifixion, and resurrection.

After this discourse on such a serious topic, it seems strange that Salome and her sons would approach Jesus with their worship and a request. Verses 20-21 tell us, "Then came to Him the mother of Zebedee's children with her sons, *worshipping Him, and desiring a certain thing of Him.* And He said unto her, 'What wilt thou?' She saith unto Him, 'Grant that these my two sons may sit, the one on Thy right hand, and the other on the left, in Thy kingdom.'"

Such a difference this worship of Salome from that of Mary of Bethany! Salome worshipped, but with a request for power and position for her sons. Even though Jesus had just told them what He was going to experience in Jerusalem, nothing was offered, no oil for His burial, no tears for the washing of His feet ... nothing. There seemed to be no realization of what He was going to suffer, or of their need to bow before Him because of it. The worship of Salome, James, and John, at this point in time anyway, was colored with self interest while Mary's worship was all about Jesus.

It is interesting to note that both events drew the displeasure of the other disciples. Jesus corrected them in both instances. In Matthew 26:10, Jesus said to the disciples concerning their criticism of Mary's worship, "Why trouble ye the woman? for she hath wrought a good work upon Me." In Matthew 20:24-28, Jesus explained to the ten disciples who were indignant against the request of James and John, that greatness in His kingdom is determined by service, not position.

Is there any wonder why Mary of Bethany's worship was so precious to Him? It was so precious, in fact, that He memorialized Mary and her worship forever.

In John 4, Jesus makes some concrete statements about true worship. He was sitting at Jacob's well waiting for the return of His disciples, who had gone into the city to buy food. A woman had come to draw water, and Jesus began to share with her about her life and living water. She perceived Him to be a prophet and brought up the subject of worship in a certain location.

Jesus replied to her by saying in verses 21-24:

> "Jesus saith unto her, 'Woman, believe me, the hour cometh,
> when ye shall neither in this mountain, nor yet at Jerusalem,
> worship the Father. Ye worship ye know not what: we know
> what we worship: for salvation is of the Jews. But the hour
> cometh, and *now is*, when the *true worshippers* shall worship
> the Father *in spirit and in truth*: for the Father *seeketh* such
> to worship Him. God is a Spirit: and they that worship Him
> *must* worship Him in *spirit and in truth*.'"

Mary of Bethany was just such a worshipper. She was keenly aware
of her past condition and her present Saviour. This awareness kept
her in a place of true humility and adoration before Him. She never
considered position or power; only how wonderful He was and how
worthy He was of worship. My, how He must love this combination.

48

Thou Art an Offense unto Me

J esus sent word to John the Baptist in prison about His ministry. He added almost as a postscript, "And blessed is he, whosoever shall not be offended in Me " (Matthew 11:6). Do we ever consider what we do that might offend Jesus?

In Matthew 16:21-28, Jesus explains what is offensive to Him. He began to explain to His disciples exactly what would happen to Him in Jerusalem. He said emphatically that He *must* go there and suffer many things. He would be killed and then raised again on the third day.

Of course, we know what came next after He revealed this to His disciples. Peter took Jesus and actually began to rebuke Him, saying, "Be it far from Thee, Lord: this shall not be unto Thee" (Matthew 16:22). Jesus must have had His back to Peter, for verse 23 says that He turned and said unto Peter, "Get thee behind Me, Satan: thou art an *offence* unto Me: for thou savourest not the things that be of God, but those that be of men." Not savouring the things of God is an offense to God. When we put the things of men before the Lord, we are an offense to Him.

At that particular time, the things of God that should have been of extreme value, were the impending crucifixion, death, burial, resurrection, and ascension of the Lord. Great events, cataclysmic events, were about to take place. The old covenant was about to end, and the new covenant between God and man was about to be cut with the redeeming blood of God's true Lamb. Rocks would rend. Darkness would fall. Devils would screech. Angels would watch in awe as the Father bruised His precious Son, allowing things to happen to Him that they could not understand, or receive for themselves. The union between Father and Son would be sliced open with sin's knife and placed in the ensuing gap ... the eternal soul of humankind.

These things, yes, these things were to be savoured! They still are. The disciples did not understand these things even though Jesus told them over and over what was going to happen to Him. We live in the "afterward" of the cross; however, sometimes we don't savour these glorious things ourselves, or I don't think we would so easily "neglect so great a salvation".

49

Time

Time to me is an enigma. It is a puzzle indeed. It holds us in its grip. We order our lives by it. We earn our income by accomplishing tasks during its prescribed duration. We measure healing and aging by it. Time sits like fruit on a tree ripening, then bursting forth into something it never was. We wait, often longingly, for it to pass. When it does pass, we can't believe it has!

The scripture in Genesis 4:3 gives us a great explanation of "time". It says, "And in *process of time* it came to pass, that Cain brought of the fruit of the ground an offering unto the Lord."

Time is the process. Events are prepared for us, and we are prepared for and by them. Time is the cooking pot. Time is preparation. Time is God's great tool. Just like a stew simmering on the stove, there comes that moment when it is ready, or it will overcook. The fruit on the tree grows in size and flavor until that precise moment of peak ripeness. If not consumed then, it will begin the process of decay. Time has its fullness.

Paul tells of the great example of time being full when he said in Galatians 4:4-5:

DONNA LEWIS ABRAMS

"But when the *fulness of the time was come,* God sent forth His Son, made of a woman, made under the law, To redeem them that were under the law, that we might receive the adoption of sons."

The Saviour came at the precise time in history, the exact moment of ripeness in God's eternal plan, to achieve His purpose: the Perfect Man, flawless at the peak of manhood, was consumed. He was manifested at God's precise moment in time (1 Peter 1:18-20).

Another astounding fact in the scripture concerning "time" is found in Revelation 10:5-7. This chapter is detailing some of the activities God's mighty angels will be carrying out in the last days. John states:

"And the angel which I saw stand upon the sea and upon the earth lifted up his hand to heaven, And sware by Him that liveth for ever and ever, who created heaven and the things that therein are, and the earth, and the things that therein are, and the sea, and the things which are therein, that *there should be time no longer:* But in the days of the voice of the seventh angel, when he shall begin to sound, *the mystery of God should be finished,* as He hath declared to His servants the prophets."

God's mystery ... finished! Completed! Present! There will be no more waiting for things to happen. Of course, this is why there will no longer be the need for time. The process will be complete! We will be living in the great eternal now.

Once I heard a young preacher express this quite wonderfully. He was preaching from 1 Corinthians 13 and brought out this same truth as veiled in verses 12-13. Paul said:

"For *now* we see through a glass, darkly; but *then,* face to face: *now* I know in part; but *then* shall I know even as also I am known. And *now* abideth faith, hope, charity, these three; but the greatest of these is charity."

When time is no more, there will no longer exist the need for faith or hope. All will be fulfilled. The process, the waiting will all be completed. Only love will exist, which, of course, is why love, or charity, is the greatest of the three. God who is love, will be all in all.

Paul gives us this completion in 1 Corinthians 15:24-28, where he says:

"Then *cometh the end,* when He (Christ) shall have delivered up the kingdom to God, even the Father; when He shall have put down all rule and all authority and power, For He must reign, till He put all enemies under His feet. The last enemy that shall be destroyed is death. For He hath put all things under His feet. But when He saith all things are put under Him, it is manifest that He is excepted, which did put all things under Him. And when all things shall be subdued unto Him, *then shall the Son also Himself be subject unto Him that put all things under Him, that God may be all in all.*"

Time will be no more! All will be fulfilled, and we will be living in the great eternal present!

50

Treasures in Darkness

When we think of light and darkness, we usually post good and evil to them respectively. Then we read scripture and have second thoughts. In Psalm 139:12, scripture reads, "Yea, the darkness hideth not from Thee; but the night shineth as the day: the darkness and the light are *both alike to thee*." And again in Psalm 97:2, "Clouds and darkness are round about Him: righteousness and judgment are the habitation of His throne."

Jesus Himself said in Matthew 10:27, "What I *tell you in darkness*, that speak ye in light: and what ye hear in the ear, that preach ye upon the housetops." It is important to note here who is doing the talking and when ... Jesus is telling us things in darkness. Only when we are walking in the light, do we need to speak of these things.

When we find ourselves in a situation, or set of circumstances, that baffles our understanding, when darkness seems to close us in on every side and we just can't seem to see a clear way of going, we need to stop, be still, and know.

Darkness is just absence of light and not always evil, as we are so quickly prone to think. Consider taking your rest in sleep ... have you ever tried to sleep in a room full of bright lights? Hard to do! There is a great rest, a deeper rest achieved by yielding to God in the darkness *until* He divides the light from the darkness, just as He did at the dawning of creation. He calls the known from the unknown, the light to shine out of the darkness.

Here in the place of stillness, of total rest in God, here in this place come the … "treasures of darkness and hidden riches of secret places" spoken of in Isaiah 45:3. Here, in your silence unto Him, He speaks to you to "be still and know" that He indeed is the eternal, sovereign God, even in the midst of your immediate darkness.

Listen! The whispers that come in His still, small voice will compound inside your heart as a precious ointment to be poured first on Him and then upon the lives of others. What you have heard in the darkness, you will then be enabled to speak in the light. Others will "take knowledge of you that you have been *with* Jesus" (Acts 4:13).

There is a great difference between learning things about Jesus and learning things from Jesus. It is good to learn things about the Lord, and in the early stages of our walk of faith, we need this. These are the searchable things that Bible studies, good books, and Christian speakers can give us. However, there are the "unsearchable riches of Christ," which Paul refers to in the book of Ephesians 3:8. These are not learned from books or any other source. They come from union with the Lord, from His Spirit to our spirit, and no other way. We may experience this in private, or in the presence of others while gathered together unto Him. They usually come during times of difficulty when we just simply do not understand why things are as they are, when His presence seems hidden from us; His voice seems to go silent, and scripture appears useless.

In Ephesians 3:17-19, Paul so beautifully sums up these treasures by holding out to us this:

> "That Christ may dwell in your hearts by faith; that ye, being rooted and grounded in love, May be able to comprehend with all saints what is the breadth, and length, and depth, and height; And to know the *love of Christ, which passeth knowledge,* that ye might be filled with all the fullness of God."

Unsearchable riches, treasures, hidden riches of secret places, so often come from times of darkness when we don't understand His ways, but we trust His heart.

51

Underneath Us

Deuteronomy 33:27 reads, "The Eternal God is thy refuge, and *underneath* are the everlasting arms ..."

What a wonderful thing to have everlasting arms under us, not just embracing us. Consider the difference. Embracing arms express love, tenderness, concern, and joy. We remember the adage of a few years back that questioned, "Have you hugged your child today?" How wonderful it is to know this love of Christ!

Arms that are "underneath" and "everlasting" imply a different concept. They speak of a strength that doesn't tire. We can hold a baby for only so long until our arms give way. We may want to continue, but we have a limit. Everlasting arms support us when we have gone as far as we can go. When we reach our limit emotionally and physically, then we often find what Hebrews 4:9-11 calls "God's rest". We discover those wonderful, everlasting arms that lend support with no strain, when we simply have reached our immediate limit. They never tire!

Those everlasting arms are also there to break our fall, to stop us from plummeting into what scripture frighteningly calls the "depths of Satan" (Revelation 2:24).

This same idea is also expressed in Romans 14:4, which says, "Who art thou that judgest another man's servant? to his own master he standeth or falleth. Yea, he shall be *holden up:* for God is able to *make him stand."* God is able to hold him with His everlasting arms until he is able to go forward on his journey once again.

With that thought in mind, here is a good place to read all of Deuteronomy 33:27: "The eternal God is thy refuge, and underneath are the everlasting arms: and He shall thrust out the enemy from before thee; and shall say, 'Destroy them.' "

No matter how far you think you have fallen, Friend, the arms, the Everlasting Arms, are under you ready to stop the fall. Knowing this, understanding this kind of blessed love, helps us to grasp the meaning in Romans 2:4: " ... the goodness of God leadeth thee to repentance." Yes, the goodness of God *leads* to repentance and the "sorrow of God works repentance" (2 Corinthians 7:10). Thank God for those everlasting arms underneath us!

Psalm 139:7-10 expresses the thought of His arms holding us so beautifully when it reads:

> "Whither shall I go from Thy spirit or whither shall I flee from Thy presence? If I ascend up into heaven, Thou art there: if I make my bed in hell, behold, Thou art there. If I take the wings of the morning, and dwell in the uttermost parts of the sea; Even there shall Thy hand lead me, and Thy right hand shall *hold me."*

Even Christians may think they have gone too far. We may believe our sins are too terrible, or our weaknesses just too difficult to overcome, but I tell you, absolutely not! Underneath you are the *everlasting arms*. Those arms were stretched out at Calvary. They willingly accepted spikes and spit, torture and tearing in a temporary surrender to weakness as Jesus *became sin for us*.

Sometimes we squirm and twist in those arms. We want to jump out and run off on our own like frightened animals. We resist. We rebel. We "kick against the pricks" (Acts 26:14). All the while, the Lord waits patiently for us to tire out, and give up the struggle against Him. He waits for us to "enter His rest" (Hebrews 4:9). There is great power to be found in God's rest.

The *everlasting arms*, in the person of God's ascended Christ, have a power and strength about which we can only stammer, and to which we remain surrendered in glorious rest.

52

Watching in Expectation

The ministry of John the Baptist involved road building; preparing the way upon which the Lord would travel. His ministry involved explaining to the people what repentance and remission were all about. The people were steeped in the old covenant ways; John was laying the groundwork for the new and living way.

John's father, Zacharias, prophesied concerning his son in Luke 1:76-77:

> "And thou, child, shalt be called the prophet of the Highest: for thou shalt go before the face of the Lord to prepare His ways; To give knowledge of salvation unto His people by the remission of their sins."

In Luke 3:8-17, John the Baptist spoke to the people about bringing forth fruit that would demonstrate true repentance. As the people questioned him about this, John became more specific about such fruit. He explained in verse 11 about giving basic things to those in need, such as clothing and food. He instructed publicans to be fair in tax collecting. He told soldiers to be less violent, more honest, and content with their wages.

Verse 15 gives us a wonderful sense of the readiness of the people for the Lord's perfect arrival time. It reads, "And as the people *were in expectation*, and all men mused in their hearts of John, whether he were the Christ or, not; ..."

The people were *in expectation*. They were looking for the Lord. They were watching for the promised Messiah. When John came on the scene, it was only natural that they wondered if he could possibly be the One promised in scripture. They weren't just waiting; they were expecting it to happen and in their lifetime. What a difference!

How sad it is that when the very One sent from God came to them, they knew Him not, though He fulfilled all the scriptural prophesies openly among them.

One of the most poignant moments in the life of Jesus comes in Luke 19:41-42. Jesus had made His triumphal entry into Jerusalem on the back of a donkey. His disciples had praised God with a loud voice for all the mighty works they had seen. The Pharisees had admonished Jesus to rebuke the people for their praise. Jesus had replied that if these held their peace, the very stones would cry out.

And then, verse 41 says, "And when He was come near, He beheld the city, and *wept over it*." Jesus cried. He cried when He looked at Jerusalem, and He said, "If thou hadst known, even thou, at least in this thy day, the things which belong unto thy peace but now they are hid from thine eyes" (Luke 19:42).

How terribly sad. How terribly, terribly sad. This was their day, their time to receive the Messiah, and the majority of the Jews missed it. Their expectation ended in refusal. Jesus knew it would, and it broke His heart. He had desired to gather them together as a hen gathered her brood under her wings, but they would not (Luke 13:34).

The apostle Paul also spoke of "waiting in expectation" when he wrote in 1 Thessalonians 4, concerning the return of the Lord to this earth. No greater teaching could be given concerning this second coming than what Paul said in verse 17 when he simply used the pronoun *"we"*.

Paul said in verses 16-17:

> "For the Lord Himself shall descend from heaven with a shout, with the voice of the archangel, and with the trump of God: and the dead in Christ shall rise first: Then *we* which are alive and remain shall be caught up together with them in the clouds, to meet the Lord in the air: and so shall we ever be with the Lord."

Paul said, "we"! He included himself as present and alive when the Lord should come again. Paul fully expected this event to happen in his lifetime, or he would never have used the pronoun *"we"*! Now, that is watching with expectation!

Are we looking for Him this way, living as though at any moment we could hear His shout, hear the trump, and be caught up into the air to meet the Lord?

No one will miss this event, not this time! We are told in Revelation 1:7 by John, "Behold, He cometh with clouds; and *every eye shall see Him*, and they also which pierced Him: and all kindreds of the earth shall wail because of Him. Even so, Amen."

For the Christian, no event is more welcomed than the second coming of our Lord. We should all be *watching in expectation*!

53

We Can Do Nothing Against the Truth

In 2 Corinthians 13:8, Paul made a strong, emphatic statement when he said, "For we can do nothing *against* the truth, but *for* the truth." We can do nothing against the truth, for the truth is not a system of belief. The Truth is a person who now sits on the right hand of God in the heavens.

Jesus declared in John 14:6, "*I am the way, the truth, and the life*: No man comes to the Father, but by Me." Can't get any clearer than that.

Man's attempts to prove truth otherwise are like the efforts of a gnat hurling itself at a granite rock in the futile hope of budging it. Truth is fixed. Truth doesn't change. Men and politics change. Both may try to say something against the truth. They may call good evil and evil good, but the truth doesn't change because of their words or actions.

However, we can do something *for* the truth. We accept the truth. We agree with the truth. We allow truth to change us. We can express the truth, or allow the truth to be expressed through us. We can express truth by the manner in which we live our lives. Our lives can be lived in such a way that men will "ask you a reason of the hope that is in you" (1Peter 3:15).

How wonderful to know in these perilous times of shifting sand, there is One who is the same yesterday, today, and forever. No man, no principality, or power in heaven, or on earth, no circumstances or events can change Him. He is exalted on high, sovereign God triune, ever living to make intercession for the saints and orchestrating His plan for the ages to come with precision and perfect timing. *We can do nothing against the Truth.*

54

We See Jesus Crowned!

As Bible-believing Christians, we know Jesus overcame sin, death, and the grave. We believe He is part of the triune God. We believe He always existed with God before time began, and that He was present and instrumental during creation (Colossians 1:16-17), (John 1:1-3), (Romans 11:36).

Christians believe that in the fullness of time, God sent forth part of Himself, His son, to be born of a virgin, to live the life of a sinless man in a human body, to taste death for mankind, reconciling all men everywhere to God by the willing sacrifice of His own holy life.

We believe death lost its grip on Him. He arose! He arose in a glorified body! He arose as the last Adam, now glorified, exemplifying the body changed from terrestrial to celestial becoming the first of a new kind of God Man equipped to rule and reign in a new heaven and on a new earth wherein will dwell righteousness.

Oh, glory be! And we shall be like Him for we shall *see Him as He is*! We believing Christians will also be changed "in a moment, in the twinkling of an eye" (1 Corinthians 15:51-54). As we have borne the image of the first Adam, so shall we bear the image of the

Second Adam, the Last Adam, Jesus Christ, the Lord from heaven (1 Corinthians 15:45-47). Seeing Him *now,* as *He is,* is everything, and seeing Him as He is means we understand this about Jesus:

> "Who being the brightness of His glory, and the *express image of His person,* and upholding all things by the word of His power, when He had *by Himself* purged our sins, sat down on the right hand of the Majesty on high; Being made *so much better* than the angels, as He hath by inheritance obtained a more excellent name than they" (Hebrews 1:3-4).

The book of Hebrews gives us such glorious truth encapsulating the very essence of who Jesus, the Christ of God, is. Yet, it also is very honest with us as well about our present limitations.

In Hebrews 2:8-9 scripture says:

> "Thou hast put *all things* in subjection under His feet. For in that He put all in subjection under Him, He left *nothing* that is not put under Him. *But now we see not yet all things put under Him,* But *we see Jesus,* who was made a little lower than the angels for the suffering of death, *crowned with glory and honour;* that He by the grace of God should taste death for every man."

As long as we age and die, we do not see all things put under His feet. We cannot deny that sickness, aging, and death exist. Faith, prayer, and scripture will not make them evaporate, but His second coming will! When that great event happens we too shall see and experience *all things put under His feet, as He does now.*

However, until that day, when death takes our loved ones, *we see Jesus crowned!* When old age robs us of health and strength, *we see Jesus crowned!* When world events trouble and vex us, *we see Jesus crowned!*

When trials and tribulation scoff at the very things we believe, *we see Jesus crowned*!

Paul declared this glorious truth when he stated in 2 Corinthians 4:8-18:

> "We are troubled on every side, yet not distressed; we are perplexed, but not in despair; Persecuted, but not forsaken; cast down, but not destroyed …"(8-9). "While we look not at the things which are seen, but at the things which are not seen, for the things which are seen are temporal; but the things which are not seen are eternal" (v. 18).

To the Christians who will be alive on the earth during the events foretold in the book of Revelation, seeing Jesus crowned will carry them through whatever amount of tribulation, if any, they may be called upon to experience, understanding that it is Jesus Himself who will loosen the seals and set these cataclysmic events into motion (Revelation 5:1-14). It is He who gives the power to the angels to carry out God's orders. Yes, it is Jesus Christ indeed who will do these things for *He is crowned sovereign Lord of All!*

55

When Jesus Appears Differently

" **T**hen took they up stones to cast at Him: but Jesus *hid Himself*, and went out of the temple, going through the midst of them, and so passed by." (John 8:59)

> "And behold, two of them went that same day to a village called Emmaus, which was from Jerusalem about threescore furlongs. And they talked together of all these things which had happened. And it came to pass, that, while they communed together and reasoned, Jesus Himself drew near, and went with them. *But their eyes were holden that they should not know Him*" (Luke 24:13-16).

> "But Mary stood without at the sepulchre weeping: and as she wept, she stooped down, and looked into the sepulchre, And seeth two angels in white sitting, the one at the head, and the other at the feet, where the body of Jesus had lain. And they say unto her, 'Woman, why weepest thou?' She saith unto them, 'Because they have taken away my Lord, and I know not where they have laid Him.' And when she had thus said, she turned herself back, and saw Jesus standing, and *knew not that it was Jesus*" (John 20:11-14).

What is our response to be when the Jesus we think we know suddenly appears to be very different, or hides Himself completely? How flexible are we when the One we have always accepted as He, is suddenly altered and no longer fits into our mindset?

Just when we think we have an understanding of how He works, the One who changes not seems to throw a monkey wrench into our precious plans, and we are left gasping for spiritual air, or scratching our biblical heads in complete amazement.

We think we have it all down into a pat formula. We have our scriptures lined up to support our thinking; then, out of the blue, something new is thrown into the mix, and everything is skewed. At this very point is where believers either become disciples and launch out into the deep, or remain near God's shoreline with their feet in ankle-deep water.

> "And it came to pass about an eight days after these sayings, He took Peter and John and James, and went up into a mountain to pray. And, *as He prayed, the fashion of His countenance was altered, and His raiment was white and glistering*" (Luke 9:28-29).

Well now, this was certainly a very different-looking Jesus! He glistened! And there with Him were two men who had been dead for hundreds of years, Moses and Elijah! What a shock all of this must have been to Peter and John! What would we have done? Probably we would have done just as Peter did, run off at the mouth and make plans to use human activity to house a spiritual happening. Build tabernacles for all! Won't work ... ever.

Then comes the cloud, God's fog; everything is suddenly different ... the glistening is gone. They cannot see as they did. Fear grips Peter and John, and now comes that Voice.

God *speaks out of the cloud*! God tells them what they need to do. "This is my beloved Son: *hear Him*" (Luke 9:35).

Jesus spoke of the importance of this when He quoted Deuteronomy 6:3-4 in Mark 12:29-30. A scribe was pressing Him for the first and most important of the commandments. And Jesus answered him by saying:

> "The first of *all* the commandments is, '*Hear*, O Israel; The Lord our God is one Lord: And thou shalt love the Lord thy God with all thy heart, and with all thy soul, and with all thy mind, and with all thy strength: this is the first commandment ...'"

Jesus tells us in Matthew 13:16-17 just how blessed we are if we have eyes to see and *ears to hear*. He further tells in Revelation 3:20-22, how important it is to hear His voice, and open the door so He can come in and sup with us. Following the hearing, opening, and supping, Jesus adds in vs. 21-22, "To him that *overcometh* will I grant to sit with Me in My throne, even as I also overcame, and am set down with my Father in His throne. He that hath an ear, *let him hear what the Spirit saith unto the churches*."

When Jesus appears differently, or even seems to hide, it is those who have learned to hear, open, and sup with Him, who know what it means to "eat His flesh" and "drink His blood". They understand "following the Lamb whithersoever He goeth". They grasp and live the premise of "dying to self", and have heard and answered the call of Psalm 42:7, which says, "Deep calleth unto deep at the noise of Thy waterspouts: all Thy waves and Thy billows are gone over me." These are the overcomers who recognize the Lord's voice no matter the puzzling circumstances of His appearance (Revelation 12:11). Oh, Lord, give us all understanding in these things, so we may always be ready to receive You no matter how You appear.

56

Why Haven't You Mourned?

Paul was very upset over a "commonly reported" incident that took place in the church at Corinth. Sexual immorality was happening in the church. Repeatedly, believers had been warned that sex outside of marriage was not just a sin against God, but also a sin against their own bodies. Paul reminded them, and us, in 1 Corinthians 6:15-20 that our bodies are the temple of the Holy Spirit. We are bought with a great price and should glorify God in our bodies and in our spirits. The same most certainly holds true today.

Yet, in Corinth a man, a brother in Christ, had actually taken his father's wife. Paul addressed this very seriously with a strong letter of correction. He went so far as to advise the church in Corinth to "deliver such an one unto Satan for the destruction of the flesh, that the spirit may be saved in the day of the Lord Jesus" (1 Corinthians 5:5). Paul admonished them not even to keep company, or eat with a fellow believer, who openly, without shame, engaged in this, as well as other spurious behavior.

What strikes me as dangerous to the church in all this, however, is what the apostle Paul said in v. 2, "And ye are puffed up, and *have not rather mourned …".* You have not mourned. You have not mourned! In other words, this awful act did not even bother you. You accepted it without so much as a backward glance.

Are we mourning today? Are our hearts aching and breaking and mourning over the lifestyles and habits of many of the Lord's people? The Quakers used to pray for the gift of tears. Do we? There are some strong indications in scripture that we should be mourning … actually trembling, along with the mourning.

In Ezra 9, we see God's people mingling themselves with false religions and engaging in pagan practices. Ezra, a Jewish scribe and a priest, fell on his knees and in verse 6 said, "O my God, I am ashamed and blush to lift up my face to Thee, my God: for our iniquities are increased over our head, and our trespass is grown up unto the heavens." Do we mourn? Are we collectively ashamed of what is happening among many believers today?

In Ezekiel chapters 8-9, God took His prophet up between earth and heaven to the city of Jerusalem and there He showed Ezekiel what was happening in His holy temple.

In verse 6, God said to Ezekiel, "Son of man, seest thou what they do; even the great abominations that the house of Israel committeth here, that I should go far off from my sanctuary? …" (His Spirit left.) False idols were everywhere. Even the elders of the house of Israel were doing dark things in their secret chambers saying, "The Lord seeth us not; the Lord hath forsaken the earth" (v. 12). Women sat weeping for Tammuz, a false god of food. Men turned their backs toward the Lord's temple and faced the east, worshipping the sun.

In Ezekiel 9:4, God gave instructions, apparently to His angels, to … "Go through the midst of the city, through the midst of Jerusalem, and set a mark upon the foreheads of the men that *sigh and cry* for all the abominations that be done in the midst thereof." Those who had mourned over the sins of God's people, would be spared in the coming judgment.

Lest we comfort ourselves by saying that all these things were under the old covenant and we are under the grace of the new, we need to prayerfully consider some tough New Testament scriptures that are seldom preached in the church today.

For example, in Hebrews 10:26-31, scripture says:

> "For if we sin *wilfully* after that we have received the knowledge of the truth, there remaineth no more sacrifice for sins, But a certain fearful looking for of judgment and fiery indignation, which shall devour the adversaries. He that despised Moses' law died without mercy under two or three witnesses: Of how much sorer punishment, suppose ye, shall he be thought worthy, who hath trodden under foot the Son of God, and hath counted the blood of the covenant, wherewith he was sanctified, an unholy thing, and hath done despite unto the Spirit of grace? For we know Him that hath said, 'Vengeance belongeth unto Me, I will recompense, saith the Lord.' And again, 'The Lord shall judge His people.' It is a fearful thing to fall into the hands of the living God."

Romans 11:21-22 reads:

> "For if God spared not the natural branches, (Jews) take heed lest He also spare not thee. Behold therefore, the goodness and the severity of God: on them which fell, severity; but toward thee, goodness, *IF* thou continue in His goodness: otherwise thou also shalt be cut off."

Hebrews 6:4-6 reads:

> "For it is impossible for those who were once enlightened, and have tasted of the heavenly gift, and were made partakers of the Holy Ghost, And have tasted the good word of God, and the powers of the world to come, If they shall fall away, to renew them again unto repentance; seeing they crucify to themselves the Son of God afresh, and put Him to an open shame."

Revelation 22:19 reads:

> "And if any man shall take away from the words of the book of this prophesy, God shall take away his part out of the book of life, and out of the holy city, and from the things which are written in this book."

Now, those are some serious scriptures. I did not write them. Some say they refer to Jews. I don't see how Hebrew 6:4-6 could possibly be speaking of anyone but believers. When have you heard them preached? Lately? Not likely. We tiptoe around these texts because they frighten us. They confuse our theology. I believe in the assurance of salvation. All I can say is, whoever these people are, I don't want to be with them. Maybe what the church needs today is a good dose of the reverential fear of God … a holy respect and awe that will help us to remember that, yes, He is a holy God, and even the Lamb has "terror" (2 Corinthians 5:11).

We know that believers may fall into terrible sin, awful, horrible, sin. But if those Christians are true believers, they will not continue in that sin. They will not feel good about it. They will hate it. The Holy Spirit will see to that. Unfortunately, if believers do not respond to the Holy Spirit's conviction with godly sorrow and repentance, then the result is a slow hardening of the heart, and eventually, a "conscience seared with a hot iron" (1 Timothy 4:1-2).

Without question we see the sad effects in believers' lives when they partake of the Lord's communion while practicing willful sin. The warning in 1 Corinthians 11:29-30 is very clear and serious. "For he that eateth and drinketh unworthily, eateth and drinketh damnation to himself, not discerning the Lord's body. For this cause many are weak and sickly among you, and many sleep." Does this mean everyone who is weak, or sickly, or who dies is living in sin? Of course not! Those who are practicing willful sin know who they are most assuredly.

Thank God for His grace! There is no depth of sin into which we can go that the grace of Jesus Christ cannot reach. Apparently, the man who had the wife of his father discovered this, and was restored successfully to the faith. However, Romans 6:1-2 tells us, "What shall we say then? Shall we continue in sin, that grace may abound? God forbid. How shall we, that are dead to sin, live any longer therein?"

Oh, Lord, "Let the priests, the ministers of the Lord, weep between the porch and the altar, and let them say, 'Spare Thy people, O Lord'" (Joel 2:17).

57

Why Jesus Is Hated

Scripture tells us plainly why Jesus was, and is, hated. Jesus spoke of this hatred Himself in John 7:6-7. His brethren wanted Him to make public declaration of who He was, but Jesus told them in verse 6, "My time is not yet come: but your time is always ready. The world cannot hate you; but Me it hateth, *because I testify of it, that the works thereof are evil."*

The words of Jesus remove all cloaks. Every pet sin and personal preference is disclosed. All self-defense is shattered. Every thought, motive, and intent of the heart lies opened. Pretense and pride surface. Flesh shrieks and demons howl. Nothing escapes exposure when holy light shines upon it. Holy light makes men hide and demons plead.

When Holy Light shines with its convicting power of revelation, men will do one of two things: they will fall before God for the covering of righteousness provided by the atonement of Jesus Christ, or they will lash out in hatred, whether vocal or silent, against the Deliverer. There are no exceptions.

The scripture speaks clearly of this in Hebrews 4:12-13:

> "For the word of God is quick, and powerful, and sharper than any twoedged sword, piercing even to the dividing asunder of soul and spirit, and of the joints and marrow, and is a discerner of the thoughts and intents of the heart. Neither is there any creature that is not manifest in His sight: but *all things are naked and opened unto the eyes of Him with whom we have to do.*"

Yes, every last detail of open and secret sin is revealed shockingly to us in a flash of brilliant truth. That is conviction. That is the "horror of great darkness" spoken of in Genesis 15:12 before God made a covenant with Abraham laying the groundwork under the old covenant, that Jesus would fulfill in the new. The light first exposes, then offers cleansing and covering for what is revealed. This is salvation!

Jesus tells us in John 15:18-19 that the same world that hates Him will also hate us. He said:

> "If the world hate you, ye know that it hated Me before it hated you. If ye were of the world, the world would love his own: but because ye are not of the world, but I have chosen you out of the world, therefore the world hateth you."

Be prepared for this hatred. As the darkness intensifies, as more and more fence-sitting Christians wane in their testimony, true believers will shine brighter. The brighter the light in them shines, the more sin is exposed by contrast. The more of Christ's life that is expressed, the greater will be the reaction of hatred. Those who live godly in Christ Jesus *shall* suffer persecution (2 Timothy 3:12-14). This is particularly difficult when you find opposition to Christ within your own family (Matthew 10:34-36).

Jesus gives the end-time signs in Matthew 24:4-51. In verse 12 He tells us that because iniquity shall abound, the love of many shall wax cold. He then tells us in v. 13, to "endure", in v. 20, to *"pray"*, in v. 42, to "watch", and in v. 44, to *"be ready"*.

May the Lord not only give us strength to endure, but also grace to be overcomers spoken of in the book of Revelation. It helps us to remember that His kingdom is not presently of this world. The kingdom of God is now *within* us (Luke 17:21). The kingdom of God is righteousness, peace, and joy in the Holy Ghost (Romans 14:17). Amen!

58

Ye Know Not

In Luke 9:51-56, Jesus set His face steadfastly to go to Jerusalem. There was a steel resolve in Him to go. His purpose for coming into the world lay in Jerusalem. He understood what was going to happen there, and told His disciples what would take place.

The greatest event in the history of humankind was about to happen. The stage was set. The players were in position. Angels were on tiptoe. Deceased prophets and saints were waiting in great anticipation. Demons and devils were trembling. Son of Man and Son of God was about to enter Jerusalem on a divine mission from God. The Father would allow the bruising of His Son. He would put Him to grief (Isaiah 53:10). The precious blood of God's Perfect Lamb would be horribly shed, and tenderly carried to the heavenly mercy seat. Man's final redemption would be completed. God would provide *Himself* as a lamb. Something of all that was about to happen showed on His face and demeanor, and the expression of His strong resolve amazed His disciples and bothered people.

In Luke 9:52-53, Jesus sent messengers before His face to enter a Samaritan village to make ready there for Him. However, they refused to receive Him there because "His face was as though He would go to Jerusalem" (Luke 9:5). Jesus was set in His purpose. They saw it and were troubled.

In verse 54, when James and John, who wanted to be greatest among them, saw the rebuff of the Samaritan village, they wanted to command fire to come down from heaven to consume them. How dare these common people refuse the Lord, *and them, entry!*

However, instead of rebuking the Samaritan people, the Lord turned and rebuked James and John soundly, "Ye know not what manner of spirit ye are of. For the Son of Man is not come to destroy men's lives, but to save them" (Luke 9:55-56). No big deal to Jesus. No big deal to the man who was about to sacrifice His life for these very people. No harsh words for them. He simply went on to another village.

We make such big deals out of so many things. We just don't know what spirit we are of. *We know not.* The most outstanding event in history was about to happen, and in the face of refusal, Jesus calmly said, "We'll go to the next village." Mercy on us, Lord, have mercy.

59

Yoked with Christ

I n Matthew 11:28-30, Jesus says:

> "Come unto Me, all ye that labor and are heavy laden, and I
> will give you rest. Take My yoke upon you, and learn of Me;
> for I am meek and lowly in heart: and ye shall find rest unto
> your souls. For My yoke is easy, and My burden is light."

Jesus never questions that life can be, and is, hard, back-breaking,
gut-wrenching work. He never says we won't have tremendous
burdens to bear, or awful heartbreaks to endure. He simply tells us
to come to Him, not to our friends, or spiritual guides, not to our
books or past successes, just to Him … Himself. He does not qualify
the call. He says if you are burdened, overpowered, at the end of your
rope, come, all of you; come to Me.

The amazing thing about being yoked with Him is, although the
yoke restricts, it also liberates. How can this be? What a paradox …
liberation within restriction!

We find the same analogy located in other scriptures such as Luke
17:33, where Jesus says, "Whosoever shall seek to save his life shall

lose it; and whosoever shall lose his life shall preserve it." Losing leads to preservation just as restriction leads to liberation.

Jesus was yoked. He was one with the Father. He spoke in John 5:17, saying, "My Father worketh hitherto and I work." He made it even more plain in John 5:19, when He said, "Verily, verily, I say unto you, The Son can do *nothing of Himself*, but what He seeth the Father do: for what things soever He doeth, these also doeth the Son likewise." He moved in unity with the Father. If the Father moved, He moved. If the Father stayed, He stayed.

Five beautiful times in John 17, Jesus prayed to the Father that His followers might be *one* with the Father and with Him. He longed for us to have union, oneness, to wear the liberating, gloriously restricting yoke of union with Him and the Father.

The writer of Hebrews calls this yoke the "rest" of God. Hebrews 4:9-11 tells us, "There remaineth therefore a rest to the people of God. For he that is entered into His rest, he also hath ceased from his own works, as God did from His. Let us labour therefore to enter that rest ..." There is the paradox again ... laboring to enter into rest.

Our greatest labor is to cease, to surrender, to stop the self-effort, to simply come unto Him. Successful service in the eyes of God is birthed from union, oneness with Him and His Son, not from anything else. No matter how grand the effort, or result, anything born through the flesh remains flesh. Only those things done through the Spirit, with the Spirit, and in the Spirit carry the breath of heaven ... the evidence of the "yoke".

Lightning Source UK Ltd.
Milton Keynes UK
UKOW05f2345150617
303415UK00001B/162/P